SEASONED LIFE
LIVED IN
SMALL TOWNS

Memories, Musings, and Observations

To Kris —
May my stories
evoke many happy
memories of your
own.
Janet Sheridan

JANET B. SHERIDAN

outskirtspress
DENVER, COLORADO

A Seasoned Life Lived in Small Towns
Memories, Musings, and Observations
All Rights Reserved.
Copyright © 2013 Janet B. Sheridan
v2.0

Outskirts Press, Inc.
http://www.outskirtspress.com

ISBN: 978-1-4787-0240-5

PRINTED IN THE UNITED STATES OF AMERICA

Table of Contents

Part 3 Fall

Part 4 Winter

Preface

I will live out my days with seasons. I need the new beginnings signaled by the determined emergence of daffodils, the comfort of an ascendant sun, a floating leaf of crimson, and a sky swollen with snow.

I like standing with my face tilted to the tender touch of spring, lengthening my stride and tasting the salt of sweat as I climb a sun-struck peak, feeling guilty relief when the first frost of autumn sends the flowers I've long nurtured to their little green deaths, and awakening to the raspy sound of snowplows struggling to clear the streets near my home.

I choose to surround myself with the seasons that sustained me as a child in Utah, an adult in Nevada, and a woman facing the reality of her advancing years in Colorado.

Part 1 Spring

For the residents of Craig, Colorado, spring begins when squads of high-school runners glide around melting mounds of snow; cars splash through intersections flooded with winter's run-off; and fickle winds flirt in all directions.

We watch the long-awaited season advance, struggle to maintain a presence, then scurry away to hide behind mountains still quilted with snow. As our children wear coats and gloves to hunt Easter eggs on sleet-slick grass, we grow discouraged and predict another ice age.

Then, without waiting for acknowledgement, trees blush as though embarrassed by their stirring sap; plucky shoots peek out through fading scrims of ice; and birds bustle about on home-building projects.

We are persuaded. We venture out in shorts and sandals on blustery days, telling ourselves we're not cold. Anxious to have our hands in warming earth, we put tomatoes and petunias in the ground too soon, even though we know better.

Our smiles broaden and our steps lengthen: we feel young.

Retirement and Herb's Pig

In third grade, my classmate, Herbert Peterson, claimed to have seen a two-headed pig. I didn't doubt him. In our rural area such an oddity seemed possible. He further asserted one head was good: a pleasing oink, rosy color, and kind eyes. The other was evil; it shrieked, slobbered, and nearly ate Herb's thumb.

For me, deciding whether or not to retire felt like a counseling session with Herb's odd pig. The good head talked about fewer obligations and intriguing possibilities: "You can take risks, do anything you want, run free like an organic chicken."

The evil head scoffed in disagreement: "You don't know what you want to do; you have few friends beyond work, and you're too old to run free; instead, you'll hobble about aimlessly and long for your recliner."

In the spring of 2007, two months into my retirement, I followed the advice of the good head: I walked into the Thunder Rolls Bowling Center, my heart in my throat, and found new friends in a class for beginning bowlers. Two fun-loving ladies in their thirties introduced themselves as classmates and advised, "Watch your butt out there, Hon, the lanes are slicker than spit."

They offered me a beer and asked if I thought they had a chance with the instructor. Throughout the semester, they invited my participation when they discussed their sex lives and picked fights in the parking lot. They sought my opinion about how many metal studs they should embed in which body parts. When I finally bowled above 100, they grabbed me in a bear hug and danced me around the lobby to the rhythmic repetition of their favorite profanities.

Our friendship didn't survive the end of the class: our lives were too different. But, like a bowling ball headed for a strike, my free-spirited classmates sent me spinning straight and true into my retirement. I had managed to roam free and make new friends.

Because I enjoyed bowling despite going at it like a confused spider, I enrolled in a memoir class, where I wrote stories of my childhood. I shared my efforts with positive classmates who laughed at the right times and never looked puzzled or dismayed. Encouraged, I entered a local cowboy poetry contest, won first place, and blew my twenty-dollar prize money at Mather's bar. I had discovered a passion and the courage to share it.

Finally, for the first time since childhood, I danced in public as though no one were watching. A friend insisted I join several partying women on the dance floor at a local affair. Ignoring the astonished look on my husband's face and my own lack of confidence, I shook my hips; I waved my hands; I bumped; I twisted; I shimmied down and in defiance of the odds, shimmied back up—in time to the music. I think. That night, I danced retirement's evil head out of my life.

I think I nearly fell victim to the downside of retirement because my job had consumed me. My life was career-centered and goal-oriented: another degree to earn, position to seek, skill to develop. Others might retire, but I would work. When I died, my classroom would be enshrined, and a plaque hung: "Janet Bray Bohart Sheridan taught here."

Then I grew weary, knew I must retire, and did. I spent the first two months of my retirement like an angry teenager: flailing about for an identity and recoiling from the responsibility of planning and executing meaningful activities to fill my days. I retreated into sloth: over-eating, over-sleeping, and substituting novels for life.

Fortunately, retirement's good head, my head, persevered and forced me to climb out of my recliner, take classes—and dance.

Quite a Family

The windows of the crowded chapel stood open to a June day of abundance in 1954 as the unfamiliar bishop with lank hair falling over his forehead and a gentle, buck-toothed expression stood before the Mormon congregation to welcome my family.

I felt awkward in the newness of this unfamiliar assemblage. We'd recently moved from the rural community of Lake Shore, Utah, to the nearby city of Spanish Fork. Back home, the warmth of known folks would have been washing over me. Here, the pulpit seemed too high, the music too slow, and the people a bit peculiar. The formal reading of our numerous family names into the church records would follow, a recital I dreaded: There were so many of us. The good people in attendance would think a ravaging horde had come to town.

The listing began: Vern Bohne Bray, father; Myrl Hall Bray, mother; their children: Lawrence Hall Bray, Carolyn Bray, Robert Larsen Bray, Janet Bray, Barbara Bray, Blaine Barlow Bray, and John Lanning Bray. If my mother had believed in middle names for her daughters, the deliberately paced presentation would have droned on into the next century. As it was, a plump girl dressed in polka dots turned back from the pew in front of me and whispered, "My, that's quite a family you have."

Yes, I did have quite a family: Seven children raised by hard-working parents who enjoyed us and provided for us, though not as lavishly as we sometimes wished. Seven children who laughed, fought, worked, played, broke rules, and matured in unpredictable patterns.

Youngsters who helped one another find the big dipper in the night sky, picked up books as often as today's children access the internet, and decided who would go first by chanting one-potato-two-potato. Siblings whose excitement when eating resembled the young animals they raised: appreciative noises, jostling for position, and dedication to the task.

Hundreds of miles now separate us, but we carry on our tradition of getting together every summer. A tumult of time has tumbled us into kaleidoscopic shapes, postures, and hues previously considered impossible; but as we relax into the comfort and rhythm of our relationship, the years fall away, and we continue to be quite a family.

Prayers and the Generosity
of Neighbors

A few years after my mother's death, I woke up on March 1st, her birthday, remembering the first time I was aware of missing her.

In 1946, Dad leaned over the wheel of a Chevy sedan, rocking to and fro in the seat as though the momentum of his body could force more speed from the old car. Fence posts draped with tumbleweeds appeared and vanished; the hospital with his unconscious wife receded; his destination neared—but not fast enough. The doctor had said two hours.

An erratic spring wind pushed against the car while Dad's thoughts raged against the slowness of Mountain Bell to reach rural areas and the quickness with which blood flowed from his wife's hemorrhaging body.

At the same time, Carolyn, Bob, and I huddled in our living room, dreading dinner. Mrs. Brown, babysitting while Mom went to get a new baby, believed in canned milk. We drank it with every meal she prepared. Taught to obey adults and cowed by the threatening glances of thirteen-year-old Lawrence, we forced it down; but our stomachs and our hearts were unsettled. We missed Mom.

The first lap of Dad's race finished in front of the small grocery owned by Wendell Francis, Lake Shore's unofficial mayor. Wendell maintained the document, compiled during World War II, which listed all adults in the community and their blood types. Dad needed the list: needed five donors willing to rush back to the hospital with him. Mom had received all of her type of blood the hospital had. She could die without more.

At home, Lawrence paced the room and tried to mask his worry. The canned-milk queen sang tunelessly in the kitchen. Our games faltered; even fighting held no appeal. Why did Mom and Dad think we needed a new baby anyway? And where was Dad?

With a scribbled list of potential donors, Dad plotted his route along ditch-lined country roads to find those at home. Chick Huff clambered down an electric pole and into the car with his climbing spikes attached. Old Hebe Peterson turned off his tractor and left it in the field. Three others soon joined them.

The next morning, Lawrence assembled us, sleepy-eyed and non-responsive, in the warm kitchen and told us that Dad had come home in the night long enough to tell him that Mom was really sick and would be in the hospital for a while. Our baby sister died while being born. We weren't sure what that meant to us, or how to feel about it. We feared it meant more canned milk.

As an adult, Lawrence revealed a detail he kept secret that morning: listening to Dad, trying to be brave, he asked if Mom would live. Dad responded, "I don't know." That night, for the first time, my brother prayed—not because it was expected of him in church, before meals, at bedtime—but because he needed help.

Prayers and the generosity of neighbors worked. Two nights later, we stood in the dark on the lawn of the hospital and stared up at the lit window where we had been told we could see Mom. When she appeared and waved, we returned her wave, then, self-conscious, ducked our heads. We didn't know how to respond to an image we couldn't talk with or touch.

For years, whenever we passed Hebe Peterson's farm, Dad related how Hebe shrugged off any thanks and warned: "Now, Vern, if she gets to telling bad stories and talking rough, don't you worry. It's just my blood acting up."

We would laugh, then grow quiet, thinking about the baby sister Mom planned to name Susan.

A Lesson from Loved Ones

Last spring I attended my Aunt Mary's funeral. Her younger brother of eighty-five, Uncle Norley, sat by me: his bulk diminished, his laugh weakened; his hearing reduced. As we mourned, questions about growing old swirled through my mind: questions about pain and poor health, loneliness and isolation, diminishment and death.

I never talked with my parents about their aging. I was too young and self-centered. I didn't know that one day I would have difficulty standing up from a sofa, hearing the voices of my grandchildren, and threading a sewing machine.

I wish Mom were alive so she could tell me how she handled nights when she couldn't sleep and days when her failing senses separated her from her hobbies. I wish Dad could tell me how he dealt with the slow betrayal of the work-hard body with which he supported his family. As his singing voice weakened, did he mourn the soaring tenor that used to burst from him in moments of happiness?

In the grocery story, on airplanes, at community concerts, I look at those who share my surrendering skin and ropy hands. I wonder how they cope with reluctant joints and dry eyes.

I know the one-liners: aging isn't for sissies; you're old when you think happy hour is a nap; after fifty, things wear out, fall out, or spread out. I laugh, but my questions linger. Then, on a spring day of rebirth, while listening to tender words from the pulpit about my aunt, I remembered my last conversation with her sister, my mother. I called Mom from 900 miles away the Sunday before she died. She was seventy-seven, living with heart problems, and happy.

She described her speech in church that morning; she thought she presented meaningful ideas to the congregation without droning on forever—as some do. She expressed satisfaction with a recent project: a small chest painted with graceful, red poppies. In the morning, she planned to take it to the artisan's co-op where she sold her crafts and worked on Mondays. When we said goodbye, I failed to tell her I loved her. Three days later, she died.

My mind moved on to a conversation with my dad, a man of eighty-six who still cut, hauled, and split firewood for "the old folks in town." He had talked about death: "I'm not afraid of being dead, because I'll be with your dear mother. But I do fear the act of dying. I've never done it; I don't know what to expect."

I'm grateful that my brother and his wife were with Dad when he faced what he had never done before.

Next, I thought of Adelaide, my mother-in-law, who invited me to her ninetieth birthday party. She planned to fete friends and family at a country club. She didn't golf—and didn't think much of those who did—but liked the restaurant. I asked how many guests were invited.

"I wanted to invite ninety people, one for every year I've lived, but I had ninety-eight people on my list. I decided to go ahead and invite them all. They're pretty old; we might lose some before the party." Ninety-two people, mostly friends because her family is small, celebrated this intelligent, soft-spoken, southern belle in her new lavender dress and sensible shoes.

As my aunt's funeral ended, I realized I could find my way through old age by following the examples of my loved ones: Mom's involvement with hobbies, church, community; Dad's clear-eyed look at death; Adelaide's widespread social structure; their humor. I also vowed to learn from the life of the woman we were burying, the grieving man next to me, all the good folks who helped raise me.

I stood with Uncle Norley as Aunt Mary's casket was escorted from the chapel. He put his arm around me. We leaned into one another.

Triumphant

Sometimes, when the green-bursting wonder of spring overwhelms all other considerations, I remember a childhood race.

On clean-up day, an annual spring event at Lake Shore Elementary School in Utah, students spent the afternoon outdoors: raking, weeding, collecting trash, and complaining. We tried to behave, but running wild in the sun-sweetened air of a daffodil day appealed to us much more than policing our school grounds. As the afternoon wore on, our high spirits took over, and we began throwing gravel, hitting each other with the sacks of garbage we'd collected, and hiding from our teachers behind the scraggly shrubs edging the school.

After long hours of such drudgery, the teachers admitted defeat and had everybody line up at one end of the playground for an all-school race. The principal told us to run to the far end of the field and back, then blasted on a whistle to start the stampede, while our weary teachers retired to the shade and watched for the buses that would rescue them.

As usual, I stood in a trance and didn't respond to the whistle, giving my competitors a head start. But by the time I dodged around the first graders who'd stopped to pick dandelions and touched the fence at the far end, my legs were uncoiled, and I was a front-runner.

As we neared the finish, I burst ahead of sixth-grade speedster

Howard Huff and gained on Lois Andrews, sixth-grade star. Like the little engine that could, I drew even, and then—my legs, hair, and heart flying—I left Lois behind and crossed the finish line first: a lowly fifth-grader, I had won the all-school race.

Lois pulled in behind me. She leaned over, clutched her stomach, and claimed she let me win because she had a stitch in her side, probably appendicitis. But others shouted that I'd beat her, fair and square.

My classmates celebrated my victory with exuberance and longevity—until the next day when Leon Aiken fell off the jungle gym at recess, broke his nose, and replaced me in the limelight.

Heaven Help Me

The car was crowded, the trip long, the road narrow. Conversation stalled and died. Then my five-year-old grandson Harrison fired a question: "Mom, MOM! I can't spell. I don't know how to study. What'll they do with *me* in kindergarten?"

I recognized my grandson's concern; transitions are tough for everybody. Since my retirement, I've been asked, "Now you're retired, what do you do all day?" by nodding acquaintances, third cousins, and a man discussing pansies with me at the local garden center—all of them nearing retirement age. From my own experience, I know they're really wondering about themselves.

I wish the man I married had such qualms. My husband Joel finally quit working in June of 2010. When my dad retired, he tried to rearrange Mom's cupboards, took up knitting for a week, and mailed his offspring articles touting the consumption of large quantities of raw garlic. I worry Joel might also lose his bearings.

Most of our conversations about his retirement revolve around activities he will no longer have to do: manage diverse personalities, keep early appointments, attend rambling meetings, shave. When he mentions new interests, however, his notions astonish me.

He hopes to augment our food supply by fishing. I like fish, but how much of it can be done day in and day out in a Craig year? Perhaps during winter he could stock an aquarium and dangle bits of hamburger from a string, though I might have trouble eating a guppy. He wants to vary his fitness routines by originating exercises to work his facial muscles. He studies me as he expresses optimism about reducing sagging skin through cheek, forehead and chin calisthenics.

He threatens to write letters to the editor. He is in the habit of sharing colorful vocal opinions about local, state, and national events with me or, in my absence, the TV news anchors. Now he wants to publish his judgments. I like living in Craig. I don't want to have to move or wear a disguise.

Uneasy about Joel's plans, I am prepared with suggestions—if he should ask. He could slow down and enjoy small pleasures like showering. After I retired, I began to savor my daily dunking, because it was no longer necessary to see how quickly I could run the old buggy through an automated wash and dry. Similar surprises await Joel. He has been navigating the workplace freeway for thirty-eight years; now he'll have time for worthwhile detours.

He could perfect how he listens and responds. To me. He can be an entertaining conversationalist, but when he thought about his job, he would answer in single syllables and look at me without recognition, let alone adoration. I anticipate his retirement, when we can have more of the intimate, in-depth, rambling conversations we enjoy.

He could try a new activity, something he would need to practice: falconry, origami, ballet. Again, I have a selfish motive. Joel does many things well; perhaps if he once again experienced imperfect beginnings, he'd be more impressed with my novice attempts. Last winter I clicked cross-country boots into impossibly narrow skis, grabbed poles in a death grip, and shuffled forward, my body stiff and frantic, a robot on speed, chanting, "Kick-glide, kick-glide." I thought I deserved hallelujahs for my exertions. Instead, when I forced Joel's feedback with a direct, earsplitting query about how I was doing, he responded, "Decent."

Perhaps both my worries and my self-serving suggestions are unwarranted. This morning, as I sat in my living room writing, I looked out the window at Joel. He stood in spring sunshine, watching birds flock to the feeder he had replenished. He seemed happy, in the moment, open to the day.

What am I fussing about? My husband will bring to his retirement, the same qualities that served him well throughout his life—intelligence, curiosity, appreciation, humor. He'll be fine. So will I. So will we.

Sleepless Nights

I discard clothes and curios of faded importance without hesitation: an ashtray from Reno, a Yellowstone T-shirt, a TWA shoulder bag; but my decisiveness deserts me on sleepless nights when past transgressions march around my head. I toss, turn, and try to delete memories of my selfish actions, hurtful words, and self-believed lies, but cannot; so I stumble to their accusatory cadence on my feet of clay throughout an endless night.

But, sometimes, I remember Les: He slouched into my third-period freshman English class in early March, his last stop before expulsion, and dragged a desk to the back of the room. His acne-scarred face flamed red, and his angry eyes dared me; then he lowered his head and pretended to sleep. I ignored his behavior and taught class.

Sometime during his second week of sullenness, he raised his head and appeared to follow the lesson—though he contributed nothing and avoided my eyes. The next week, he laughed with the class when a frustrated student complained that the only part of a short story she enjoyed was "The End." Soon he began handing in adequate assignments, contributing during discussions, and passing tests. He had a C at mid-term, but continued to reject my friendly overtures.

In April, between the noisy departure of my third-period students and starting on the stack of papers I planned to correct during my planning period, I walked to the back of the room to close a window. As I passed Les's desk, my foot slid through a sickening puddle of tobacco juice. I knew Les chewed because of the faded circle on the back pocket of his jeans, so I went to his next class and asked for him. "Les, go to my room right now and clean up the disgusting mess you left by your desk." He followed me without complaint, gathered paper towels, cleaned the carpet, and then approached my desk.

To my surprise, he established and maintained eye contact. Seeing no sign of insolence or anger, I explained I would report his behavior if he defaced the classroom again and sent him back to class. The rest of the year went by without incident.

After the dismissal bell on the last day of school, I was sitting in my classroom, savoring the quiet, when Ronny—known for his musical ability and sneakiness—stuck his head in the door: "Hey, Mrs. Bohart, remember when you marched into science and made Les clean up the chew in your room? He didn't spit it there. I did. Gotcha!"

Ronny ran out of the building, and I went looking for Les. I didn't find him. When I tried to call his home to apologize, the number was no longer in service. Another regret joined the throng that paraded in my mind when I couldn't sleep.

Several years later, as I shopped at a chain drugstore in Reno, a tall young man with a shy smile and an assistant manager's nametag approached, stopped in surprise, and said, "Mrs. Bohart! Wow!! I can't believe it's you."

I read the name below the title and blurted: "Les, oh, Les! I've been hoping to run into you for eight years. I need to apologize; I accused you of something you didn't do and made you clean up someone else's mess. I found out too late that you didn't do it; Ronny did. I am so sorry."

"Hey, no big deal. You treated me fairly from day one—actually made me like English—and besides, I did so much bad stuff in junior high, it didn't hurt me to clean up someone else's chew."

We chatted about his promotion at the drugstore, his wife, and their new son. As we parted, he thanked me again for helping him salvage his ninth-grade year. I felt the peace of his forgiveness seep into my soul.

Sometimes, memories of Les save me from my sleepless nights.

Rare Sightings

When I can't see what others point out to me, why do they act as though I'm apathetic, irksome, or dull-witted? I have trouble distinguishing distant, miniature objects. Does that mean I'm peculiar? I don't understand why my inability to discern far away items causes others to tear their hair and yell. While they jabber and gesticulate, I do my best to locate the bird, animal, star, person, or plant causing the commotion. I concentrate, pop my eyeballs, and scan vigorously side-to-side, up-and-down, round-and-round. I become woozy, wild-eyed in my frenzy to see, but never hear "nice try" or "better luck next time."

Last spring, a great horned owl perched in our blue spruce for a couple of days and announced its presence by hooting. "I can't believe you don't see it," Joel said, "It's there. Right there. There where those two parallel branches extend from the trunk. See it? Right there! THERE!!!"

Well, thanks, Joel; repeating the same words at increasing volume while waving your hands around like a whirligig is extremely helpful. Finally, the kind bird noticed my plight, pitied me, and flapped its wings until I found it and put a stop to Joel's agitation.

My problem with seeing wildlife is persistent. When my family moved from Utah to Wyoming after my high school graduation, everyone in the car exclaimed over the herds of antelope bounding with grace and spirit on the horizon. After long minutes of silent scrutiny, I thought I had one in sight and marveled aloud at its speed. Sharp-eyed Blaine snorted and announced to one and all that I had sighted in on a squashed insect on the window.

When I married Joel and moved to Colorado, I thought he had a snipe hunt in mind when he insisted there were mountain sheep along I-70 near Georgetown. For years, going to and from Denver, I wondered what character flaw made him want to belittle me. Then one bright day, a ram stuck its head over the cement barricade on the side of the road and introduced himself. Now I'm the first to sight the creatures—though sometimes I point out odd-shaped boulders.

I've always wondered why so many of the games we play involve balls we have to track. I've never heard anything more useless than the advice that echoes around baseball diamonds everywhere: "Keep your eye on the ball!" How, pray tell, does one do so?

Coaches and teachers also yelled another inanity at me: "Watch 'er into your mitt, Janet, watch 'er in." Excuse me? I lost track of the ball when it left the pitcher's hand and had no chance when the batter belted it my way. I spent my softball-playing years standing in center field, hoping the inning would end before a ball flew into my territory.

I'm always last to see stars and constellations, even when peering through a telescope during a college astronomy class under the direction of the teacher. While others sighted Vega, Orion and Cassiopeia, I wrestled with my telescope and prayed for cloud cover. The instructor sighed and moved on.

So, tired of arousing impatience and ridicule in others, I've taken up lying. After a suitable interval of searching in vain, I exclaim, "Oh, I see it!" then quickly follow with a generic comment spoken sincerely: "Wow, amazing, isn't it? I can't believe it."

I think Joel has caught on. He's begun asking pointed questions about the bird I claim to have located: "Is the ring around its eye yellow or white?"

Well, how the hell should I know? I can't see it.

Memories On Mother's Day

In the end, my mother died as she lived, with resolution and strength. After all, you do what you have to do.

As a teenager in the fifties, I discovered many things I didn't want to do, things potentially embarrassing or difficult. I whined about these distasteful tasks, badgering my mother to excuse me, rescue me. I couldn't ride the ancient, rusted, family bike to band practice. It had only one pedal and jungle rot. Everyone would laugh.

Why did I have to pick tomatoes to pay for the Jantzen sweater I wanted? Did Mom understand the humiliation of crawling along those endless, muddy rows? Of dodging tomatoes the seriously sick Fillmore boys launched at my butt?

"I know I'm the one who told Bucky Boyle I'd go to the dance with him. But he has huge red freckles, even on his lips, and smells like a barnyard. Couldn't you call and say I've come down with polio?"

Mom would suffer my harassment only so long before turning from an ever-present task: "Janet, you know what you need to do. Now quit wasting time and do it." Those oft-used words signaled the end of her patience and the discussion. With varying degrees of speed and grace, I eventually did as she said, because I knew she practiced what she preached.

When I was twelve, fire destroyed our family home and many of our belongings. The piano burned; few toys survived. Jars of fruit representing hours of sticky labor exploded. Bedding used to fight the fire was ruined. Clothing suffered smoke damage, and nice china shattered. Mom had seven children, no home, essentials to replace, a meager budget, and a husband made angry by his inability to "keep a roof over the heads of my kids."

When I picture my mother during the fire's aftermath, I recall unending work, a resolute look, a head held high, and a don't-you-dare expression when any of us complained about missing toys or clothing.

When I was thirty, I stood next to Mom in an overgrown cemetery near Grass Valley, California, amidst a whirling of insects and emotions. We had driven from my home in Nevada to visit the gravesite of Mom's second child, Alan of the perfectly shaped eyebrows and happy demeanor, who died at two from whooping cough. "Mom," I asked, "how did you keep going after such a loss?"

"I did what I had to do," she replied, "but I mourn him to this day. I still dream I'm walking through sunshine in a vast meadow of flowers. I hear Alan calling me, but I can't see him. I search with my heart in my throat, but don't find him. When he died, I couldn't give in to my sorrow. I was a young wife trying to make a home from a tarpaper shack in a mining town. A husband working long, dangerous hours and another child depended on me. I had no nearby family to help. I kept going."

At seventy-seven, this practical woman, who dreaded becoming a burden to her family, talked happily with the children who called or dropped by her house on Sunday. She died three days later in the hospital. My brother JL who was with her described her demeanor in the moments before she died. He said in the darkness of a long night, he saw the determined "Mom look" we knew so well creep over her face and watched her bring all the power of her considerable will to her last task, clamping down hard on his hand. Our mother died as she lived, with determination and dispatch.

So I believe that when her children face the lonely act of dying, we'll hear her voice: "You know what you have to do. Now, my child, it's time to do it."

Destroying Dust Balls

Last year, I didn't get around to spring housecleaning until November. By then, I'd lost my enthusiasm and toiled in misery. Now, it's April, and I'm in a quandary: Because I spring-cleaned in November, it seems too soon to tackle it again; and do I want to be inside clutching a bucket and scrub brushes while daffodils flirt with spring breezes and sudden blizzards? On the other hand, the destruction of elusive dust balls during the month of Thanksgiving seems to miss the point of spring-cleaning. I haven't been this conflicted since I fretted about whether I should start asking for the senior discount I deserved.

I inherited my reservations about cleaning from my grandmother. She once counseled me to accept the fact that a woman's work is never done. Then we hung rugs on the clothesline and whacked the dickens out of them. I remember her words and lament the repetitive nature of housework whenever I push a howling vacuum or wash grimy walls. Routine weekly cleaning takes the better part of a day. Then, twenty-four hours later, crumbs crunch underfoot; toothpaste decorates the basin; and grease splatters besmirch the stove.

My mother made certain her daughters possessed housekeeping skills, but my sisters and I never managed to whistle while we worked. When she couldn't escape, however, Carolyn tackled cleaning tasks with impressive vigor, making me look like an ineffective sluggard.

A neighbor, Mrs. Bradford, once hired me to clean her house when Carolyn moved on to a better job. Mrs. Bradford wore thick glasses and moved slowly around her gloomy house; so I thought I could get by with casual cleaning— "a lick and a promise" in Grandma's words.

Wrong. Carolyn set the bar too high, and, falling victim to her mean streak, she "forgot" to warn me about my new employer. My first day on the job, Mrs. Bradford told me about Carolyn getting on her hands and knees to clean mopboards with a toothbrush. She then waddled behind me, rubbing a white handkerchief over areas I had cleaned and holding it to the light, looking for dirt smudges. "Janet," she lectured, "your sister understood that any job worth doing is worth doing well. What happened to you?"

It was a three-handkerchief day.

My disgruntlement with cleaning increases when I have to purchase supplies. I'm perplexed by all the options: Supermarket shelves offer twenty alternatives for dusting. And when did we decide we had to slaughter every little bacteria lurking in every little cranny? My eyes go blurry before I manage to read all the small print outlining the uses, virtues, dangers, remedies, and directions for each product. So I buy the last thing I touched.

Growing up, we cleaned with a limited arsenal. Spic and Span in water was our all-purpose tool, supplemented with Dutch Cleanser when necessary. Toilets were scrubbed with noxious blue granules— and fortitude. I'm certain the gel we spread with a little brush to dissolve scabrous droppings in our oven had enough toxicity to kill canaries. We may have cleaned with pollutants, but we didn't dither when purchasing supplies.

Recently, a friend shared a liberating thought with me that I'm thinking of tattooing on my wrist: You don't have to clean the way your mother did.

Graduation Distress

Last year I sat in crowded bleachers with a multitude of proud, camera-toting families at my granddaughter's high school graduation. From the "Pomp and Circumstance" entrance to the mortarboard-tossing finale, I enjoyed her ceremony more than any of mine.

My commencement disappointments began in ninth grade. We girls walked into the hall in twosomes and joined another female duo to promenade the center aisle, interspersed with quartets of adolescent boys resplendent in new suits and Old Spice after shave, whether it was needed or not. As a teacher monitored the girls' line, she realized we had too many starch-stiffened petticoats under our voluminous skirts, and, walking four-across, we would wipeout any inattentive or feeble occupants in the aisle seats.

We waited twenty minutes as male teachers, sweating in suits and ties, removed chairs from each side of the aisle. This bustling activity displaced parents who had arrived early to get aisle seating so they could take better photographs of their graduates. Folks were disgruntled; fisticuffs were threatened. Mr. Beckstrom, a large man, worked diligently to remove chairs and referee arguments, then passed out. Fifteen more minutes went by while he was revived and carted off.

Because of these set-backs, I had less time to cavort with Kirk Halgrimson at the graduation dance—Dad had to get home to milk the cows before his night shift. How glamorous.

In high school, the girls of my class were the first in the history of the school to walk with boys of a similar height, rather than their boyfriends. The principal decided the class of '61 would march in like a rope of pearls strung small to large, because he was tired of mediating the spring hullabaloo over who would walk with whom. Thus, I promenaded with Roland Gunderson, the tallest boy in the class—a nice person, but no Elvis.

The decision to have the graduates write and present a pageant rather than listening to a guest speaker also broke with tradition and caused personal disappointment: I wasn't asked to be on the script-writing committee. Mr. Davis said graduation was a serious occasion with no need of sophomoric humor.

I represented the teaching profession in the pageant. I fussed about how to costume myself before deciding I'd wear glasses, lace-up shoes, and a shapeless dress; I carried books and tried to look wise. Scotty Baker asked why I hadn't worn a costume.

I next attended a two-year junior college, graduated with an associate's degree, and astonished both the audience and myself as a student speaker. Between farewell dates with my true love, I wrote a speech and memorized it. Misjudging my mental capacity, I carried no notes with me to the podium. Halfway through, I ran out of words: "My fellow graduates and I have benefitted...My fellow graduates...My......"

What an impressive sight: eyes bulged, mouth agape, mind blank. Mom looked horrified. Dad hung his head so low his chin rested on his ankles. The graduates stopped daydreaming and swung their tasseled heads toward me in startled unison, like a covey of quail. I still flinch when I remember the silence as twenty seconds crawled by while I stood mute, trying to reconnect with my mind.

Two years later, I marched six blocks in a procession across the campus of Utah State to my graduation ceremony. The evening before, showing off in my cap and gown, I cooked dinner for those family members who'd traveled to Logan to see how I'd embarrass them this time. As a result, the smell of fried catfish wafted from my robe as

I toppled along on heels too high for a forced march. The last two blocks, I hobbled on blistered feet among my fish fumes—and delayed the entrance of the entire College of Education.

Graduation speakers talk about the joy of the occasion and the pride of the accomplishment. I wouldn't know.

Rest and Recreation

A breeze flowed damp and heavy through open windows and across the crowded baggage area. I followed its tropical smell, looked out at rain-sparkled Hawaii, and remembered the Salt Lake City airport, six months before. There, below autumn-washed mountains, my first husband, Bill Bohart, walked away from me and toward Viet Nam.

Tomorrow, April 21, 1968, I would see him again. The army called their program R&R, and soldiers tracked their progress toward it on shaded short-timer calendars decorated with drawings of lightening bolts, peace symbols, and jungle trails. With each filled-in date, a soldier drew closer to the end of his time in Viet Nam. An intermediate goal, usually achieved after six months, was a week of leave for rest and recreation with loved ones in Hawaii or other selected sites.

I collected my luggage and boarded a bus waiting to provide hotel transport for women who had flown from across the United States for non-stop recreation and little rest. That night at the Outrigger Hotel, I worried. I'd heard about a woman who arrived at the R&R welcome center to meet her husband and was instead met by kind-eyed officers with soft voices: "Mrs. Smith, could you come with us, please?"

My last letter from Bill had arrived ten days ago.

The next morning, wearing false eyelashes, black eyeliner, a mini-skirt my parents would never see, and hair teased into an impossible bubble, I walked into the jeweled daybreak of a misty island and caught a cab to Ft. DeRussy, in the heart of Honolulu. I joined approximately 150 women who radiated perfume, nervous laughter, and instant friendliness; most of us having done out best to look like Priscilla Presley.

A staff sergeant addressed us. He said our husbands could be nervous, moody, or withdrawn. They might be angry, unable to sleep, or unwilling to talk about where they had been, what they had seen, what they had done. They could cry—often and unexpectedly. It might take a few hours or even days for them to become more like the men we had kissed good-bye. "But," he assured us, "you will be the best thing these guys have seen in a long time. You're beautiful. And they're about to tell you that, themselves. Their buses are arriving."

A communal intake of breath nearly sucked him from the stage. Tears flowed. As instructed, we formed two lines, four-feet apart, extending from each side of the door the men would enter. The sergeant patrolled the lines, making us laugh by mimicking our anxious behavior: giggles, fresh coats of lipstick, repairs to tear-damaged mascara.

A young wife next to me hyperventilated. Another applied a fresh layer of Tabu perfume. Someone let out low, pained bellows, reminding me of our heifer Sweet Alice when she gave birth. A wild-eyed girl with her hair lacquered high chanted repeatedly: "I've forgotten what he looks like; I've forgotten what he looks like. My God, we were only married three weeks; I've forgotten what he looks like."

A bus appeared outside the open door.

The first men to walk the gauntlet of panting females looked tired, dazed, and uneasy. They had been pulled out of action twenty-four hours before. Now they faced 150 bedecked bundles of hormones surging toward them, whooping, moaning, and crying. They entered tentatively, one by one, their eyes searching, and smiles blazing when their wives ran into their arms.

While joyful reunions occurred around me, I fought back worry. Where was my husband? All the men had buzz-cut hair; many were tall and slender. None of them were Bill. The last bus emptied, and I feared the approach of gentle officers. Then I saw him.

As always, Bill looked cool, unfazed, and in control; but the blue eyes that riveted mine told a different story.

Playing Like Children

As a grandparent, I've laughed, moaned, and cheered while watching soccer, T-ball, softball, basketball, volleyball, track events, and swim meets. I've been indignant, amused, ecstatic, nervous, resigned, and bored out of my mind. I've sweated sunscreen from my face, struggled to sit upright in unrelenting gales, huddled under blankets to ward off humid cold, and run away from lightening tugging toddlers—all so I could reassure my grandchildren that I saw their hit, score, or outstanding play.

Along the way, I've stored up vivid memories: Lucy as a senior digging a volleyball off the court and returning it during championship play; Sophia with a baton and a determined look out-running the older girls; Sally staying in her own lane at a swim meet—most of the time—and Harrison kicking a soccer ball that, much like Old Faithful, regularly went straight up in the air and straight back down.

But my best memory of grandchildren at play is watching their impromptu kickball game on a Sunday afternoon on an Illinois day of daffodils and sunshine. They used their cast-off jackets as bases and enforced their few rules haphazardly, depending on the age of the player: Young ones kicked until they connected; older ones changed positions and sides at will. Thorough discussions conducted with loud voices and vigorous gestures resolved disputes, and play continued.

PLAYING LIKE CHILDREN

Do you remember free-spirited play organized by you, your siblings, and your friends or cousins? Games that lasted until bedtime? Games played without uniforms, spectators, officials, or coaches? Games played for fun, not parental approval?

I do; and many of the memories revolve around my oldest brother. One late spring afternoon, Lawrence assembled four of us—Carolyn, Bob, Barbara and me—on the front lawn. Then, with great drama and suspense, he explained the rules to a unique baseball game he had invented: Barbara and I, the youngest, were to serve as officials while he would pitch to Bob and Carolyn. He bragged he would strike them out every time and coaxed them to bet huge sums of money they didn't possess against his ability to do so. As, in turn, they assumed the batting stance they'd learned from him, his strategy became clear.

He threw high balls, wide balls, inside balls, bouncing balls: pitches they couldn't possibly reach. After each outrageous toss, Lawrence asked six-year-old me to make the call: ball or strike. He had whispered to me before his first throw that a strike was a good thing and a ball was not, but I had no idea how to distinguish the two. So he helped me.

Ignoring Bob's shrieked laments and Carolyn's fierce protests, he kindly explained what I saw until it became clear to me that this pitch, like all the others, was a strike.

When Bob and Carolyn threatened to quit if he continued to cheat, Lawrence agreed to seek a second opinion from Barbara, age two. He approached her, nodding his head up and down, over and over, as he asked, "It was a strike wasn't it?"

Barbara, wearing a diaper and dirt, interrupted her pursuit of ants to consider the matter. Then, slowly and gravely, a miniature Buddha, she duplicated his exaggerated nods. The cuteness of her actions caused triumphant cackles from Lawrence, uproars of indignation interspersed with giggles from the batters, and relief from me. Then the game, played by children for fun, continued.

Through A Window

"Hey, Janet, you watching animal movies this spring?" my brother Blaine asked with a stifled laugh.

"Yes, and I suppose you're looking for animals to shoot," I replied. I'd explained to my incredulous brother several springs before that my favorite part of the season was early mornings in my living room with Joel and a cup of coffee, watching animals frolic in our yard. I described squirrels bouncing across the grass, tussling with one another like rambunctious boys looking for trouble, while sparrows, siskin, and finches swooped in for an early breakfast.

"Before long," I continued, ignoring Blaine's amused reaction, "robins splash in the birdbath, fawns peer through the fence, hummingbirds argue around their feeder, and butterflies drift above flowers open to the sun."

"Sounds like a Disney movie," he responded. "Good for you; you've managed to surround yourself with the little critters you always adored: Bambi, Thumper, and the bluebirds that wrapped ribbons around Cinderella."

"Tell me," he added when he stopped laughing at himself, "do the little birdies ever fly into your windows and break their little necks?" Blaine always did prefer bedlam, but I don't let his ridicule deter me. I continue to be rewarded by my dawn window-watch.

THROUGH A WINDOW

Joel and I hang our birdfeeders in early April. Soon excited sparrows, the busybodies of the bird world, discover the feeders and spread the word. The next day, numerous birds fly in through the morning light to feast at our diner. Squirrels try to join them at the table, but can't. We bought our feeders because their packaging didn't claim they were squirrel-proof, only squirrel-resistant. We appreciated the honesty.

The first time we hung one of the new feeders, a squirrel circled it, preparing for a dare-devil trip along thin aspen branches, down a swaying wire, and onto the feeder—the outer case of which is supposed to slide down under the squirrel's weight, thus covering the openings where birds perch and snack. After long minutes of hanging by his toes and exploring all options, the squirrel abandoned the effort and leaped away, acting like it wasn't interested. Fifteen minutes later, it reappeared, climbed the tree at breakneck speed, stretched its Gumby body long and thin until it reached the feeder's top, then swung the rest of its body over. The holes snapped shut. Joel and I high-fived.

This year, a raven decided our yard had possibilities. He paced the length of the sidewalk, flipping pieces of bark out of our border of mixed perennials like a prankster overturning neighborhood garbage cans. Then he discovered the birdbath and stalked about in it for a few minutes before flying away. Moments later, he returned with a piece of stale bread, obtained from some other feeding station, dropped it in the birdbath, and took leisurely bites of the softened bread: a ritual he repeated every day for a week before moving on to new adventures.

A toddler hummingbird charmed us one summer by perching perilously on our telephone wire every morning, shedding baby down and looking confused. We picked up several miniature fluffs of feather from beneath his daily perch before he groomed himself to perfection, figured out his purpose, and took flight.

I remember hearing in school that many fascinating animals exist in our world, but most of us ignore all of them except those that could harm or feed us. That would be true of my brother Blaine, but I prefer the animals in the Disney movie I watch through early morning windows every spring.

A Gentle Holiday

As we noisily celebrate graduations and begin the rowdy rituals of summer, Memorial Day, a gentle holiday, waits for us with its quiet pleasures. Instead of festooned presents, rollicking parties, and calorie-laden treats, our national day of commemoration offers solemn reflections, fond memories, and feelings of gratitude.

My childhood summers started softly as I helped Mom pick lilacs, iris, and buttercups, which we arranged in chipped fruit jars to leave at the gravesites of our loved ones on Memorial Day.

At the Spanish Fork cemetery, I walked with my family on new grass beneath fresh trees. We zigzagged through headstones ranging from simple to ornate and placed bouquets on the graves of the ancestors who gave us our mother. Cleaned up for the occasion and on my best behavior, I helped clear away winter's debris and listened as my elders told fond stories about our dead.

I took extra care cleaning the small headstone of Baby Bray, my little sister who died before she could be named. I smiled as I read Grandpa Hall's name on a new, dark gray headstone, because all my memories of Grandpa included laughter. But I felt unsettled, holding Grandma's hand and seeing her name etched next to his. I didn't want to think about what that meant, even after Carolyn told me to quit being a baby.

I was proud when we decorated Grandpa Bray's burial site in the Provo cemetery. He had been a stranger to me and an uninvolved father to my dad, but his grave had a small flag beside it, when most didn't. I don't remember my age when I learned the reason for Memorial Day and the meaning of Grandpa's flag, but I remember walking with Bob and my dad back to our car after leaving a jar of lilacs by his gravesite. Some men as old as my great uncles, in uniforms and strange hats, offered us small red poppies of crepe paper on a wire stem. Dad bought some and gave one to each of us.

I examined mine: "Hey, Dad, we didn't get much for our money, did we?" Dad stopped walking and told us Memorial Day began as a way to honor the brave soldiers who died fighting for our country. He said the flowers, like the flags placed in the cemetery by the Boy Scouts, helped us remember our soldiers, and we should wear them proudly. They represented something of great value—our freedom.

When Bob objected that Grandpa didn't die fighting—he died in the hospital in Salt Lake City—Dad explained that Grandpa fought in World War I and even those who didn't die in a war were remembered with a flag.

Years later, when I stood at my dad's gravesite and watched the solemnity of his military burial, I thought of his words, of the value of flags and poppies, and of a holiday that encourages us to remember those who served and the families who hugged them goodbye. I also felt gratitude that as a child I stood sturdy in a quiet cemetery under the lenient sun of May and understood my place in a long line of mostly good people.

Part 2 Summer

Summer seizes control while we sleep. After a heavy-handed winter and nomadic spring, a bright morning dawns; and the people of Craig creep into the dominance of a strong sun like moles from burrows. We blink, stretch, and move.

Bicycles circulate; foot traffic flows; yard puttering escalates. We buy too much sunscreen, free our toes to frolic in flip-flops, and wear shorts—even when we don't have the legs for them. We float boats, hit balls, hike trails, and sleep in tents. Taking advantage of the season's prolonged, unhurried evenings, we visit over backyard fences, sit on decks among pots of petunias, and walk our dogs until they give up.

We pretend summer will last forever.

Our Forbidden Playground

Beneath a sun-saturated sky, my brother Bob and I approached Utah Lake by cutting across a field at the far end of our property, crawling through a barbwire fence, and coming out on a two-track, dirt lane.

The rarely traveled path led us first to the ruins of a pump house built by our great grandfather—long abandoned slabs of concrete, partially covered by pebbled dirt and clumps of salt grass. These crumbling remains once housed a pump used to siphon irrigation water from the lake. Pride swelled in us each time we saw our ancestor's initials JH and the year 1898 pressed by his finger into one of the chunks of cement before it dried. This was 1950. We guessed his writing was at least 300 years old.

As we continued along the narrow, overgrown road, the scent of the lake enveloped us: the smell of murky water tinged with the decaying reeds and willows that grew in the surrounding marshland; an earthy smell of organic rot and stagnant water; a heavy, foreign smell that spoke to me of pirate ships in teeming ports.

Billows of mosquitoes whined overhead as we sloshed through the wetlands that skirted the lake. Seagulls flew away from our movement and chastised us for disturbing them; killdeer limped and sobbed, trying to lead us away from babies tucked into ground nests; waterfowl lifted off from the lake's surface with beating wings and quacks of indignation.

Finally, we reached the lake, its water gray-brown and dense like liquid earth, shielding carp and catfish in its muddy depths. Sometimes a wind roiled the lake's sluggishness, but mostly we found it quietly astir, slurping at the water's edge where our toes curled in thick mud.

We now had a decision to make. Would we disobey and risk consequences. Or not?

One of my earliest memories is of a burly and bald Uncle Norley demonstrating how to swim in Utah Lake: "Get around by just kicking your feet. It'll be slow, but lots more enjoyable. Keep your arms out in front of you, hands joined at the fingertips, like the prow of a boat. That will keep the big stuff away from your face. You never know when the good folks living around the lake will flush their toilets."

I didn't get it. What big stuff and what's wrong with people flushing their toilets? When I forgot to flush, I got in trouble. My uncle's words made sense to me a few years later when Bob and I, old enough to explore the countryside by ourselves, received look-at-me-and-listen-carefully instructions from Mom. We could never go to the lake without an adult, and, more importantly, the lake was not for swimming. Its water could make us seriously ill. It was contaminated.

Yet another thing I didn't understand. "What's contaminated?"

"It means that towns around the lake dump *raw* sewage into the lake's water."

Picturing strange, uncooked things, like, maybe, turnips, floating in the lake, increased my puzzlement. "What's raw sewage?"

"It's what you flush when you go to the bathroom. At our house, it goes down a pipe into a tank buried in the back yard and is stored there. Your dad puts chemicals in the tank to treat the sewage. Some people who live in small towns around the lake don't do that. When they flush their toilets, it goes into a big pipe that carries it to the lake and dumps it in without any treatment. That's why the water in the lake could make you very, very, very sick."

Well. Never mind the lake. The idea of running around outside my home, accidentally breaking through the dirt, and falling into a huge, underground tank, full to the brim with what all of us flushed and chemicals, whatever they were, scared me more than what people elsewhere were doing. Those towns were so far away that I couldn't even see them. But I, it seemed, was living on top of a pool of bathroom leavings.

Because we had been warned against it, we were tugged toward the water of Utah Lake by one another's dares, boasts and ridicule. Each time, we paused at water's edge to think about threatened punishments, far away toilets, and possibly dying from a terrible illness if we encountered the big stuff.

And, each time, we waded in.

A Man with Strong hands

I remember a robust speaker in church on Father's Day who tugged at the knot on his tie and stated with great authority and greater volume that when adults are asked to name a memorable feature of their fathers, most say, "his hands." Pleased to find myself with the majority, I nodded my ten-year-old head in agreement.

I've always liked my father's hands, though my mother may have influenced me. She believed one of Dad's most commendable qualities was his ability to open anything she handed him: jelly jars with stubborn lids; a turpentine container rusted shut; a bottle of bolts with a cross-threaded cap. "Girls," she'd say, "life's easier when you marry a man with strong hands."

I inherited my Dad's long, slender bones; but as an adult, when I slipped my hand into his, mine disappeared. His bulky, work-roughened fingers contrasted with his nickname Slim and the sleekness that marked the rest of his body. His nails were disorderly: jagged, cracked, and circled by deposits of grease and dirt. Each Sunday he did his best to scrub nails and knuckles clean before going to church, but usually gave up so we wouldn't be late.

He supported us by working with his hands in the depths of the Hoover Dam, the gold mines of California, and the iron-ore tunnels of Utah. He began as a mucker, shoveling debris, then, promoted to miner, he operated a jackhammer and handled dynamite. At thirty-five, fearing black lung, Dad left the perpetual darkness of mines to work in the heat and fire of a blast furnace at an iron mill. Sometimes hot metal burned holes in his leather gloves. Other times he came home with heat exhaustion and worried us.

When laid-off or on strike, Dad took any job he could find to prevent "going on the dole," which would be more demeaning than bucking bales in another man's field or cleaning coops at a neighbor's chicken hatchery.

At home, Dad used his hands to paint without dripping and wall-paper with precision, skills hard-taught by his unaffectionate stepfather. He pitched a curving baseball, dropped seeds into garden soil he had tilled, picked cherries by the stem as is best, bullied stubborn cows, and dealt cards like a casino worker.

I don't remember Dad ever using his hands to discipline me, except once, when he caught Bob and me playing along a forbidden drain ditch. He grabbed my shoulders and shoved me toward home, then chased Bob and gave him a whap on his backside for running away— Bob being slower than I to recognize the reality of our situation.

I also have no memory of Dad caring for me when I was little, though I know from watching him with my younger brothers that he sang to me, held me, diapered me, rocked me, and felt my feverish forehead.

I do remember the gentle touch of my father's hands and their comfort when I was a teenager. The summer before seventh grade, my family moved from Lake Shore to Spanish fork and my friendships faltered. The Lake Shore girls rode a bus to the same junior high I attended, but my church and neighborhood associations were with a group of Spanish Fork girls who had been together since kindergarten.

One afternoon, I fled into our house, told my tearful tale to Mom, then threw myself face down on the top bunk I occupied in our new home, sobbing. The Spanish Fork group I thought had accepted me had taken the train to Provo on an outing and had "forgotten" to invite me.

Dad came home from work, heard my crying, and questioned Mom. In minutes, he stood by my bed: large, work-scarred hands rubbing and patting my back. He stood silently; his hands telling me how sorry he was, how bad he felt that he had moved me from a home I loved so much.

I fell asleep to his touch; I have never forgotten it.

A Tumult of Cheese Sauce

I joined a 4-H cooking club in fourth grade so I could make stuff and eat it; then Mom decided I should make stuff and talk about it. She convinced me to prepare a food demonstration for the local fair in August and suggested I make cheese sauce. But first I'd have to learn to cook and talk at the same time.

I researched, wrote and memorized a script that extolled the virtues of dairy products, demonstrated the recipe, and suggested foods the sauce could enhance. I planned to ladle it on macaroni, green beans, and poached eggs for my grand finale. These plated-in-advance foods were rubbery by the time the sauce hit them, but my script claimed they looked "scrumptious."

Next, I practiced talking and cooking until my hands and mouth meshed. Finally, I packed tools and ingredients, polished the electric hotplate, and printed the recipe on poster board. I was ready.

I breezed through the local fair, my only competition being Billy Jo Simmons from Benjamin. Struck dumb by stage fright, Billy Jo scooped out watermelon balls in grim silence. Then, still in a soundless trance, she used toothpicks to build melon-ball animals for festive party favors. Her horse lost a leg and the bag fell off her heifer. I was a shoo-in.

For the county competition, Mom made me a ruffled apron and

trimmed my bangs. In mid-August, I stood before too many people and began: "Hi, my name is Janet Bray and I'm a member of the Nifty Nine 4-H Club. Today, I will prepare a mouth-watering cheese sauce, packed with nutrients to build strong bodies." I measured; I mixed; I smiled. I remembered every move and every word. I flourished my whisk and chuckled. Mom beamed.

Then, just as I announced that the sauce would soon boil, I realized that the hotplate had quit heating. Instead of "rich bubbles popping merrily," I stirred a freakish lump of flour and butter in lukewarm milk.

I decided to beat the blob into submission and stirred faster; my arms whirling like blades on a helicopter. I began to sweat. Adopting my father's problem-solving approach, I muttered, " Hell! What'll I do with the damn stuff?" I raised the whisk overhead and plunged it into the pot, attempting to mash the mixture smooth. Globs of milk and congealed flour splattered my apron and gummed my hair.

In desperation, I smacked the hotplate, sending it sliding into the fossilized eggs, which bounced on the floor like tennis balls. I wiped sweat, milk and flour from my eyes with the back of my arm and stared in bug-eyed panic at my mother. She slowly slashed her index finger across her throat—twice. My eyes widened in disbelief: "She has to be kidding. Why should I kill myself over cheese sauce?"

I decided to continue my presentation as planned: "I'll now pour the rich, creamy sauce into the serving dish, so you can appreciate its smooth texture." Thin milk sloshed into the bowl, followed by the re-sounding thump of the remaining coagulated ingredients. A tidal wave of uncooked sauce took out the first row of spectators.

"My, doesn't that look delicious! Notice how the golden, velvety sauce contrasts with these green beans (splat), brightens this macaroni (thwack), and would accentuate the poached eggs, which seem to have gone missing. Any questions?"

The judges commended my courage and wished me better luck next year. When Mom stopped laughing, she rubbed a glob of flour paste off my nose, and assured me I didn't have to kill myself; her gesture meant I should explain my problem and stop.

I obliged. I stopped talking for some time, sitting stonily in the car as Mom giggled and snorted, making no attempt to disguise her merriment.

I eventually recovered my sense of humor; and for decades to come, Mom and I surprised and amused one another by halting our dinner preparations to dramatically intone, "My, doesn't that look delicious!"

Herding Cats

My extended family gathered for a reunion in Wyoming in July of 2010; Joel's family convened for similar festivities in Illinois a week later. We had to depart for the Sheridan gala when my eyes were still losing focus from the shenanigans in Wyoming—but I had stopped twitching.

I have six siblings; Joel has seven. Counting children, grandchildren, family friends with more courage than common sense, and curious strangers with oh-my-God expressions, both families became multitudes—or mobs, depending on one's viewpoint.

From the initial planning to the hugs of farewell, our family reunions resembled three-ring circuses on steroids. The process of selecting a date and place begins months in advance. As specific dates are debated, calls and emails of diminishing civility are exchanged. Folks inform one another about previously scheduled functions they absolutely can't miss: dental appointments, pet spayings, the ripening of their tomatoes. When a grudging consensus on the date is reached and a head count of attendees is tallied, a site must be found. Again, bickering transpires, mostly polite.

Pity the unfortunate person whose turn it is to coordinate the selection chaos. My siblings and I noticed that being in charge of the 2010 celebration aged Blaine. During the three days we were together, we worried as he wandered around kicking tree stumps and mumbling about herding cats.

As we convened at Louis Lake in Wyoming, those late or not coming were discussed first. Some claimed Donald, absent again, would attend only if we met in his backyard; then he'd leave early. We agreed that Bessie enjoyed the attention she got every year by arriving late, claiming to be at her wit's end. Those with an altered appearance also provided fuel for commentary as we pointed out and critiqued Evelyn's tattoo, Jed's weight gain, and Gerta's enhanced chest.

Toddlers wobbled through a forest of adult legs, discarded their clothing, and explored the remains of dead animals. They rolled in dirt and cried when they were cleaned up for a nap. When no one was watching, they ran hell-bent-for-leather into the lake, causing nearby adults to stampede. They fell asleep on stairs, in the canoe, and at dinner with tendrils of spaghetti in their hair.

School-aged children clung to their parents and eyed one another shyly before responding to a signal only they recognized and running off together to play. Teenagers displayed their skill at multi-tasking: texting friends, nodding to music from earphones, discussing when they could escape, and reprimanding errant siblings.

New parents tended to their babies with a distracted air, intent on conversations with the cousins they once chased and teased. Older folks issued health bulletins, discussed retirement benefits, and remembered when they organized the softball games and encouraged the water fights. As a sister-in-law remarked while we sat and watched the hubbub around us: "Can you believe it, Janet? We've become the old aunts."

Those with strong voices issued commands as needed: "You kids quit throwing watermelon rinds!" "Whoever took Roscoe's cane needs to bring it back right now!" "Someone make Aubrey stop drinking from that puddle!" and the ever-popular, "Food's ready; there's plenty for everybody; no need to stampede and shove."

Reunion food. Oh my. Food tastes better when prepared by loved ones and eaten shoulder-to-shoulder with those who know and accept your triumphs and failures, struggles and strengths, character flaws and questionable politics. Each year, long-time relationships deepen and new ones form around tables filled with favored family recipes and multiple desserts.

Then, too soon, it's time to leave. Some carry out stealth departures, quietly drifting away to avoid the tumult of good-byes; others hug anyone who wanders within reach. A few cry; several want to. We exchange promises to keep in touch and propose vague plans for next year as cars are loaded and children wave good-by from rear windows.

And my heart overflows with gratitude for families.

A Village of Aunts

I remember playing with wooden blocks beneath a canopy of fabric stretched on a quilting frame. The sturdy hose and practical shoes of my mother's elderly aunts enclosed me; the murmur of their voices washed over me. Each held a hand on the underside of the quilt to check the depth of her stitches, causing worn-thin wedding bands to flash in the quilt's shadow. Whenever I see the word, quilting, I visualize great-aunts with swollen ankles chatting to the movement of their needles as children play in the shelter of their love.

Aunt Bertha, nearest and dearest of the great-aunts, lived down the lane from us and provided emergency services: she brought in meals when Mom was sick, baked cookies she hoped we wouldn't mind eating, and provided safe haven during trying times. One summer day, Barbara and I ran screeching into her house after escaping a bloated cow and a murderous porcupine.

"Mom's not home and there's a huge swollen cow back at our house making funny noises and foaming and trying to get through the fence to eat us," I yelled as we barged through her kitchen door.

"Yeah, it's fat and slobbery and crazy," Barbara added, "and on the way here we saw a porcupine crouching in a tree to dive-bomb us and kill us with its quills. We had to run way out into the field to escape."

Aunt Bertha stopped frying venison steak, wiped her hands on her flowered apron, and hid her amusement. She sat us at her kitchen table, gave us just enough ice cream to "fill our sweet tooth," admired our bravery and good sense, and sent Uncle Henry to investigate.

Another great-aunt, Beulah, gardened in her hustand's boots, talked too loud, laughed too hard, cussed a bit, and one day held me gently agaist her ample girth until I quit crying. An unhappy teenager, I was spending the night with her after going to a party with the Lake Shore friends I left behind when we moved to Spanish Fork. "It's not the same anymore," I sobbed. "I feel like I don't belong either place."

She said nothing, just held on and listened.

"Beulah's a bit rough around the edges," I overheard a hoity-toity second cousin remark at a family reunion.

I knew better. Aunt Beulah was soft, quiet and kind when it mattered.

Mom's youngest sister, Aunt Lois, saw me steal a piece of Double Bubble gum from a drugstore's penny-candy jar—when I was old enough to know better. "Janet, I'm disappointed in you, and your parents would be as well. Put it back." She said no more, told no one, and continued to treat me with affection. In return, I swore off shoplifting and forgave her for giving birth to Cousin Jimmy.

Mom's other sister, Aunt Mary, paid attention to me: asking about my life, laughing at my juvenile jokes, and complimenting my hair when I remembered to comb it.

When Carolyn was asked to be Miss Utah in the Lake Shore homecoming parade, I pulled the wagon which was the foundation of her royal float. Mom used dotted-Swiss fabric to make us beautiful dresses, which we modeled for our relatives before the parade. I stood beside the glory of Carolyn whose dress had a peplum—an odd ruffle around her middle—that made the ladies swoon. Unnoticed, I skulked away, feeling like an insect overshadowed by a peacock. Aunt Mary's voice stopped me: "Janet, twirl so we can see that beautiful bow on your sash." I felt like a spinning cockroach, but I twirled and smiled gratefully at Aunt Mary, who had noticed me.

I love and honor my aunts: the village that raised me.

Miss Desert Blossom

My mother often persuaded her children to try new activities we wouldn't have attempted if left to our own devices. She said our forays into the unknown would round out our personalities—and seemed to think I was in particular need of rounding.

Barbara and I, at ten and fourteen, did a comic sketch for the church talent show because Mom convinced us we needed to do something with our summer besides read and fight. She wrote and directed the routine in which we thumped out a duet on the piano, stopping occasionally to offer hilarious tidbits to the audience such as the crowd-pleasing, "Sofa to sofa and mash to mash. Don't leave your gum in your sweetie's mustache."

We should have stuck to *A Girl of the Limberlost* and sucker punches.

Mom's efforts to make a silk purse from a sow's ear peaked with the Miss Desert Blossom pageant. Each year, Spanish Fork celebrated July 24th, the date the Mormon pioneers arrived in Utah and began to make the desert bloom. In 1962, the committee in charge of the festivities decided to sponsor a beauty pageant and crown Miss Desert Blossom, who would ride with her court of honey bees on a float at the head of the annual parade of riders and horses wearing matching outfits, antique tractors belching black exhaust, and floats decorated with beauties and crepe paper.

Contestants had to be single, ages eighteen to twenty-one, and recommended by their bishops as worthy applicants. Being eighteen and free of grievous sin, I was the family sacrificial lamb. Mom bribed me by promising to sew an eye-catching dress for the competition plus two new outfits for college. I should have held out for a Cadillac.

My mother was blind to my inappropriateness for such an undertaking. She didn't see that my desert had yet to bloom, my bee to buzz. When I attended the pre-pageant meeting, I learned that every junior-prom princess, homecoming queen, and cheerleader from 1961-1964 had entered the competition. I lumbered into the room like a Winnebago at a Corvette rally. Belva Henderson, Harvest Ball Queen, 1960, reinforced my intuition when she remarked, "Oh, my, Janet, what a surprise!"

I suffered from bouts of acne, wild hair, and acute self-consciousness. I couldn't imagine "sparkling at the judges," as we were advised to do at the preliminary meeting. How does one sparkle? I tried it in front of the bedroom mirror until Carolyn asked if I'd developed a tic.

I made Barbara sneak into the auditorium with me the night before the pageant so I could practice my stair descent, the runway walk and the poses we were to strike at designated points. Staunch soul that she was, Barbara assured me that I looked cute when I stumbled on the steps. She also suggested I wear a longer skirt, because when I twirled into my poses, she could see the garters clutching the tops of my nylons.

Blaine and JL were enthusiastic in their support for me, but a bit confused about the purpose of the big event, singing, "Here comes the bride, big fat and wide," whenever I entered a room. Bob gave me brotherly advice: "Try not to look like you usually do."

The pageant exceeded my expectations by being the worst hell I have ever endured. My face burned red, my feet ached, and my hair sproinged in the humidity of my nervous sweat. Trying to maintain a smile as I lurched down the runway on heels too high resulted in a grim, stricken expression a friend later compared to death throes. As the Master of Ceremonies encircled my waist with his beefy arm and pulled me up against his prominent belly for my interview, I was so startled that I shoved him away with both hands, an action which so-licited the only laugh of the evening.

When the judges announced their decision, I was not Miss Desert Blossom, not a honeybee, not even Miss Congeniality; I wouldn't have to ride on the float. A relieved whoop escaped me, reinforcing the judg-es' decision.

Mom thought I was robbed and claimed all of her lady friends agreed. Bob acted like he didn't know me. Barbara assured me she hadn't been able to see my underwear, and Dad came out from under his chair.

Later, when I thought about the experience, I decided I'd learned a lesson: In the future, if Mom urged me to try out for the college fencing team, tap dance my way to stardom, or enter a hog-hollering contest, I would refuse. My personality was rounded.

Sweet on Sugar

Finally, it's summer, the season of cotton candy: pastel clouds of spun sugar that danced in my childhood dreams. I've been a devotee of sugar my entire life. When there were no adults around and no sweets in sight, my friends and I used to lick our index fingers, stick them into the sugar bowl that could be found in every kitchen, and lap at the clinging crystals like starving puppies. Now sugar bowls have followed the Edsel into oblivion, and my preferred ingredient stands accused of sabotaging the nation's health. Evidently, sugar is a disguised scoundrel lurking in the most unlikely of places: the sauce we enjoy with spaghetti; the crackers we serve with cheese; and the mouthwash we use to gargle.

It's been estimated that the average American consumes between 150 and 170 pounds of sugar annually. If typical, each year I eat my weight in sugar; but I exceed typical. I excel. I prefer my favorite additive as undiluted as possible: maple syrup, divinity, and Smith Brothers Cough Drops. I don't consume the sugar packets placed on restaurant tables like my dad once did—trying to get his money's worth after he saw the bill—but only because I fear the appalled reaction of my dining companions.

I linger in front of the candy shelves in grocery stores, mouth watering and fingers twitching. On a good day, I maintain my dignity and proceed down the aisle, resisting the urge to scamper back and fill my cart. On a bad day: well, I forgive myself and vow to display more strength of character next time.

I'm convinced that my addiction to sweets began while celebrating our nation's sugarcoated holidays. I devoured the spice cake Mom made for the New Year and the heart-shaped candies that read 4-U and Be Mine on Valentine's Day, and then fantasized about the marshmallow bunnies and chocolate eggs of spring. One memorable Easter, I helped Mom make sugar cookies decorated with green frosting, coconut grass, and jellybean eggs to share with my class. Before school began, I hunkered down on top of the slide with two friends, ate all the cookies, and entered the classroom with crumbs drifting my face. Later, I felt ashamed, but not sorry.

Halloween provided popcorn balls, and Thanksgiving offered a choice of pumpkin or pecan pie. Christmas was the Super Bowl of sugar: three weeks of treat-laden parties, everybody's best dessert recipes, and gifts of brownies, fudge, and cinnamon rolls in packages decorated with candy canes. I probably ate the estimated average of 150 pounds of sugar during December alone.

I supplemented our sugar-heavy holiday traditions with self-created rituals: A movie wasn't worth watching unless accompanied by Junior Mints, Necco Wafers, and 7-Up. A road trip wasn't worth taking without licorice whips and Butterfingers; a mountain couldn't be climbed without trail mix loaded with M&M's; and a birthday wasn't worth celebrating without inch-thick caramel icing on my cake.

Though prevailing wisdom decreed that sugar caused my tantrums, cavities, and acne outbreaks, I ignored advice to cut back or abstain and pursued my passion, blaming my inelegances on poor self-control, neglected grooming, and a faulty gene pool.

Recently, I read an online list of 146 ways sugar harms our health and couldn't sleep for a week. My sweet tooth could lead to cataracts, obesity, varicose veins, and premature aging. If I don't take a stand against gooey goodies, I could die fat, blind, and early with bulging veins and sugar-encrusted lips. My loved ones will view me in my casket lined with white satin and comment: "My, they did a good job. She looks so natural."

Dancing With Arnold

When younger, I struggled to control my judgmental nature: the temptation to label folks as strange, eccentric, or odd. This disagreeable tendency developed during my early teenage years when fitting in was paramount and quirks unacceptable. Adopting the prevailing mentality, I scoffed at the strange mannerisms of others and admired my flawless self.

I pursued the peculiarities of my siblings with particular care: Barbara's throat thumped annoyingly when she swallowed. Bob preferred plaid shirts. Carolyn had the ugly habit of calling me a whiner. Lawrence laughed too loud, and I couldn't understand why my mother bothered having Blaine and JL, the youngest two, who messed with my things and ate dirt.

Though Mom pointed out this unflattering weakness of mine on a schedule of her own devising, I discounted her words and went on my flawless way, gasping with junior-high girlfriends at the weirdness of others. As I aged, I became less vocal with my opinions, but still noticed aberrant behaviors when I spotted them. Then at twenty-eight, a person from my past taught me that we should withhold harsh judgments because life is not static: people change.

At my junior high in the late 1950's, students who made it to ninth grade earned a privilege—dancing lessons. From Monday through

Thursday during PE, girls wore regulation uniforms and bounded about in various games with little skill and less enthusiasm. On Fridays, we abandoned the baggy blue outfits and flocked to the gym in full-skirted dresses and clouds of Aqua Net hairspray for recreational pursuits, the term used by the school to describe our graceless prancing.

We learned outdated dances like the box waltz and polka from the angular, unhappy Mrs. Jackson and the rotund, bouncing-basketball, Mr. Henson. After their demonstration, we walked through the steps without music, paired with same-sex partners because of our attention issues. The boys refused to touch each other, which made it difficult for them to grasp the concept of partner dancing. We then paired up with the opposite sex as assigned and tried our new moves to music.

The lessons lasted until the instructors grew weary of yelling over the scratched records: "One, two-three; one, two-three, begin, two-three; one—no, no, no, no, no. Stop. STOP DANCING!" When they gave up and staggered to the sidelines, most students anticipated the next event, free dancing; but my heart sank.

Filled with foreboding, I joined the girls on one side of the gym and eyed the boys on the other. At a signal from Mr. Benson, they would quit goosing one another, cross the shoe-scuffed floor, and ask a girl to dance. I hated free dancing because when the boys charged, Arnold Evans would reach me first: thick glasses steamed with exertion and excitement, high I.Q. lost in the passion of his quest. I'd dance with a partner short enough to rest his head on my bosom, which *he* didn't seem to mind.

Arnold walked to school on hot days with a sycamore leaf inserted under the bridge of his glasses to keep his beakish nose from burning. He did scientific experiments in his basement and carried chemical burns, pungent odors, and singed hair to prove it. He told long-winded jokes with no apparent punch line. Small and uninterested, he was chosen last for teams, but on Fridays he could dash his scrawny body across the gym floor faster than any jock. He would skid to a stop, rub his hands together in anticipation, and squeak, "Come on, Janet, let's boogaloo, Babe."

He danced like an agitated puppet. I moved in rigid awareness of our uneven heights and his reputation as a peculiar, inept egghead. We were supposed to practice the dances we had learned during the year, but Arnold relied on a vague shuffle: two steps to the side, two back—over and over and over in the same spot. He danced with a blissful grin; I followed with a permanent scowl. My mother told me to be nice, but I dreaded those endless dances with Arnold.

In the summer of 1971, I attended my ten-year class reunion, my first since leaving to attend college. I huddled with former girlfriends, laughing and appraising our classmates: Natalie had surpassed pleasingly plump. Nobody could believe John's bald, bumpy head or that Darlene and Ed divorced four months into their marriage after years of smooching in the halls. And which of our classmates married that good-looking guy? Must be rich; look at his clothes. Had anyone heard whether the harvest ball queen did well in Hollywood? Probably not; after all, actresses are expected to memorize lines.

We were looking for dyed hair and purchased boobs when our conversation stopped in mid-gossip. The crowd in front of us parted, and the attractive, well-dressed stranger we'd discussed earlier approached our group. He grinned, rubbed his hands together, and murmured in a mellow voice, "Come on, Janet, let's boogaloo, Babe."

That night, I learned the lesson in humility and charity my mom never managed to teach me, as I danced, too briefly, with Arnold.

Store Up Small Things

I'm one of seven children raised by hard-working parents who supported us, molded us, and enjoyed us. During a recent family reunion, we visited our parents' grave. On a bee-buzzing summer day, we stood on gentle grass under a fresh sky and told stories of their living and their dying. Our words returned them to us, if only briefly. It's a gift to share defining details about those you love, as I realized when I visited my dad near the end of his life.

In 1999, I drove into Lander, Wyoming, mid-day on the Fourth of July. Along the small town's main street, flags waved, bunting billowed, and bars disgorged patriotic cowboys. At my parent's house, I opened the unlocked front door and lingered for a few seconds in the cool dimness of rooms filled with the essence of my mother, though she'd died five years before. Dad didn't answer my call, but I found a note from him on the drop-leaf table that slanted along with the floor of the aging home. Typically terse, his message read: "At store."

I walked out the back door and two blocks over to the supermarket. Inside its air-conditioned chill, I threaded my way through holiday shoppers buying potato chips and watched for my erect, slender, still handsome father. Then I heard a familiar sound: a series of loud deep thumps mixed with lighter hollow taps. The pattern of rhythmic knocks continued, with slightly different tones: some resonant, some muffled. I headed toward the produce section, pulled by the soft drumming only I seemed to notice.

As I brushed between the carts of women bemoaning the limp lettuce, I saw my dad. Wearing blue coveralls and a cowboy hat purchased at a garage sale, he studied a bin of watermelons. Curling his hand into a fist, he tapped his chest, tapped a promising melon, tapped his head, and then the melon again. He sighed in disappointment—the good-looking melon hadn't met his standards—and turned to thump another.

He'd taught me his secret method for selecting ripe watermelon years before: "You hit your chest twice, the melon twice, your head twice, then the melon again. Compare the sounds. A ripe one will echo the sound of your chest: deep, bass, solid. One that should have been allowed to grow a little longer will sound like your head: tinny and hollow. At least that's how my head sounds. You've been to college; it might not work for you."

Today, as I approached my ninety-year-old father, he saw me and lit with a smile, "Come over here, Janet, let's see what sort of clatter your head makes today."

We stood in the produce section and knocked away, oblivious to the glances we drew as we rapped and debated until we whacked our way to a tasty choice.

My memory of choosing watermelon with my dad has retained clarity and importance because, during those moments, I realized I could soon lose this man, and I needed to store up details about him, lest I forget.

I blinked away tears as I thumped. I don't think he noticed.

Too Secure

For many years after I married Joel, we flew to Illinois during summer vacation to visit Joel's children and grandchildren, who were the best wedding present I could have received. On one of those trips, we halted security operations at the St. Louis airport.

Our daughter had given us some tomatoes from her garden: "We've eaten so many this summer, the kids will cheer when you take them." At the airport, we placed the tomato-swollen paper sack in a bin and watched it roll past the watchful eye of the screener. We met our treasure on the other side, grabbed the bag, and turned to hurry to our gate.

Made soggy by a squashed tomato, the sack's bottom gave way. Red spheres bounced, rolled, plopped and squished. Lights blinked, buzzers buzzed, heads swiveled, and security personnel converged, yelling contradictory orders, as we bounded, stooped, caught, and corralled. Then we fled, leaving tomato stains and hostile looks behind.

I dread airport security.

As I stand in line between an impatient businessman and a befuddled family, I prepare to obey the ever-changing rules: put shoes in a bin, unless told to place them directly on the belt; remove the laptop from its case, but not the iPad; walk at will through the metal detector, or wait for an invitation.

I put thought into streamlining my passage, only to wait for travelers baffled by the bins, argumentative about removing their thigh-high boots, or carrying metal objects in every pocket—which they empty one at a time as they get beeped and turned back: again and again and again.

I went through security with my dad when he was in his late eighties. He observed carefully, and did everything correctly—until he decided he probably shouldn't wear his hearing aides through the metal detector. Before I could intervene, he ripped the expensive gadgets from his ears and threw them on the moving belt. They cleared the scanner, but dropped through the rollers on the other side and nestled in the dirt, dust balls, and debris underneath. Our crawling search-and-rescue mission held up the line and caused some passengers to grumble and complain. Dad didn't mind—he couldn't hear them.

Thanks to my pacemaker, I now play a gambling game with airline security: If I say nothing, some metal detectors don't pick it up, and I stroll on through; other machines shriek in alarm, and I have to turn back and confess. If I admit that I have a pacemaker before going through, some agents tell me to proceed; but most direct me to stand aside while they broadcast a call: "Female agent needed for hand search at security line four."

I then stand in giant footmarks painted on the floor and extend my arms to the side, shoulder height. When asked, I respond that I've been hand-searched many times before. Despite my admission of prior experience, I'm forced to listen to another detailed explanation of what Ms Female Agent will and will no do to me. "Fine," I mutter to myself, "Get on with it. Your pat down is much less intrusive than wedging myself between strangers on the crowded tram to concourse B." Ms eventually finishes her memorized litany; she then repeats it as she performs each operation, using the back of her hand in the "sensitive areas."

After making it through security, passengers enter the land of the lost: dazed fellow travelers shuffle around in bare feet, clutching their shoes, holding up their beltless pants, and dribbling dirty laundry from their hand-searched-and-not- re-zipped carry-on. Some squawk indignantly about the loss of their purse-sized hand sanitizer and others weep into their cell phones as they tell loved ones how Ms Female Agent stuck her hand down their pants.

No, my dear, you didn't listen. She merely inserted "two fingers into your waistband front and back." Get over it.

In a Split Second

Even in lives gently lived—removed from aggression, cruelty, and violence—some moments of our own making sear themselves into our memories and cling long, despite efforts to erase them. It happened to me on an August day in my early twenties: a moment that eclipsed the worries I had as I prepared my shopping list. outlived the dog I leashed as I left the cabin, and lasted longer than my marriage to the good man who waved from his work as I began my routine drive to town.

I braked for a curve on the two-lane highway running through the Sierra Nevada Mountains outside of Markleeville, California, and saw a dead motorcyclist. Only the noise of my pickup marred the tranquil scene. Weeds didn't quiver; animals didn't scurry; insects didn't dart. The Harley's back tire rotated in silence, though I thought I heard a rock skitter down the cliff looming above the road.

In a split second, I absorbed the sun-heated tar of the asphalt and the tree shadows crowding the road. I memorized the biker's scuffed boots, peaceful expression, and casual posture—one arm flung behind his head as if searching for shapes in the clouds. I witnessed dark hair un-mussed, face clean-shaven, pine trees sprinkling the road with pollen and bird song. Maybe he was napping.

Then, reluctantly, I acknowledged the truth of the slashing skid marks into the cliff. And drove on. I registered the accident—a young man hurt or dead—but didn't stop. Instead, I watched in my rearview mirror as a green government van braked and spilled rescuers; then I drove away from the man lying on the roadside.

My hands shook as I lifted items from the shelves of the grocery store; my stomach knotted as I loaded my truck with purchases. When I remembered that no other road led back to our cabin, my heart drummed in panic.

I crept back to the accident scene. Through clustered vehicles and quietly conversing people, I saw a plaid blanket pulled over a face I knew by heart. I collapsed against the wheel, my breath constricted to a rasp, my young life no longer distanced from death.

I never learned his name.

Through the years, the pine-scented scene remained with me in heart-stopping detail. Other than my husband, I told no one. For the rest of the summer, while he did his forest ranger duties—policing lakes, trails and campgrounds—I whistled up the dog, took long solitary walks, and remembered the man I came to think of as my dead motorcyclist, though I knew I had no right to claim him.

I picture death that way now, sudden serenity on a summer day.

I picture myself less kindly. Did I drive on because I didn't want to look too closely at death? Because I was frightened, worried I would be inadequate to the moment? Because the presence of others relieved me of responsibility? Or did the need to complete mundane chores eclipse my compassion for a fellow human being?

I don't know.

By writing this, I've revealed a long-held secret. But sharing my guilt hasn't cleansed me. I am older now and less caught up in the self-interest of my twenties: career, marriage, friendships and possessions. I wonder how I would react if a similar experience came my way tomorrow. Would I reach out beyond myself to others? Or would I drive by?

I sometimes ask my dead motorcyclist for forgiveness.

No More Camping

Because I had happy memories of camping as a youngster, I agreed when Joel suggested we intersperse motels with camping during our summer road trips. I must be a slow learner: it took three summers for me to realize that trying to recapture the fun of trekking through the dark of night to a smelly outdoor toilet is like trying to wear the swimming suit I wore at ten—doomed.

I remember a night in the Snowy Range of the Medicine Bow when I lay awake and worried that our bodies wouldn't be found until the August thaw. The temperature hovered at ninety-five as we drove out of town, but that night we pitched our tent on frozen ground between looming snowdrifts. After crawling into our sleeping bags fully clothed with towels and extra clothing piled on top, we slept fitfully—disturbed by the chattering of two sets of teeth and the need to massage life back into our numb noses.

The next morning, we comforted ourselves by splitting a pound of bacon.

A year later, having forgotten our frostbite, we packed for an extended trip to Glacier National Park and Canada. My cautious nature prefers reservations, while Joel thrives on spontaneity. After our first night on the ground, I crawled out of our tent in self-righteous-martyr mode.

Every campsite at Glacier bulged with children hitting each other with sticks, aromatic smoke floating from grills, and adults in flip-flops waving from their reserved spots as we drove by. So we abandoned our notions of camping and decided to get a room at the park lodge. Fortunately, before handing over a credit card, we asked to see the last room available—a closet in the basement with a door that didn't quite close, a questionable bed, and a leaking toilet.

We then thought we'd take our chances outside the park. We should have taken the swayback bed behind the boiler room. The only campground available in Babb, Montana, consisted of a pasture of thigh-high weeds bordered by posts designating twelve tent sites. Each site had an individual Sani-hut, long overdue for dumping. And nothing else. It's hard to snooze on clods and tromped-down weeds with heavy Sani-hut odors clogging your head. The next morning I didn't need bacon to comfort me; I had my thoughts: "I told you so, Mr. Spur-of-the-Moment; but would you listen? No-o-o-o-o!"

The next summer we toured South Dakota and planned two nights at Custer State Park—in a reserved site. The park boasted scenic vistas, a buffalo herd, and a refreshing contrast to the Badlands we had toured earlier: amenities difficult to enjoy on a day of record-breaking heat and humidity. Pitching a tent is an onerous task with sweat streaming into your eyes, dripping from your chin, and slicking your hands.

After dinner at an air-conditioned lodge festooned with portraits of Teddy Roosevelt and dead-animal heads, we sat in our camp chairs, stared vacantly at a discouraged stream lined by motionless trees, and dripped. When we decided to sedate ourselves with sleep, we lay on top of our bags with our arms extended and our fingers and toes spread to minimize the increased heat of skin contact. I appreciated the cleverness of my husband anew when he commented, "Hey, Janet, you'll sweat less if you don't blink."

After three camping experiences that made a colonoscopy seem festive, I finally understood: I hate camping.

Would That Be Honest?

I straightened my back, lifted my feet from the rhythmic tap of the treadle, and flexed my fingers. A whoosh of relief escaped my clenched teeth: The last buttonhole finished. Three weeks of sewing, unpicking, and re-sewing nearing an end. Next, I would snip the fabric enclosed by the buttonhole stitching, attach five buttons to my blouse, and prepare to collect a blue ribbon at the local 4-H fair.

Seizing my scissors, I folded the first buttonhole in half and pictured the gracious humility with which I'd receive my ribbon: snip, fold, snip, fold, flying fingers, fantasizing mind. Engrossed by my imaginings, I didn't notice the blouse's fabric caught in the fold of the last buttonhole.

Snip. I shook out my masterpiece and croaked with horror when I saw a triangular cut gaping open on its left side—as dismaying as a boil on a bride's nose. I wadded the botched blouse and threw it across the room, screaming that I hated to sew and would never do it again. Then, bursting with shuddering sobs, I pushed by my startled mother and ran into the hot afternoon to hide in the crushed-leaf smell at the top of my favorite cottonwood tree.

Nothing was said when I joined my family for dinner. Nothing was said as I ignored my turn to wash the dishes and stomped off to sulk in the room I shared with two sisters. Nothing was said as I pretended to read *Little Women* until bedtime. Mom, Dad, Lawrence, Carolyn, Bob, and Barbara seemed not to care that my life was ruined. I hated them all.

The next morning, at the foot of my bed, I found my blouse still warm from the iron: ruined side replaced, buttonholes finished, buttons attached. In the kitchen, I could hear my mother humming while she kneaded yet another batch of homemade bread.

I don't remember thanking Mom for my reconstructed blouse, but I do remember the fond glance she gave me as she asked if I still hated sewing. Even more, I remember the steely look that followed my reply: "Oh, no, I love it. I love this blouse. It's beautiful. It's perfect. It's sure to win a blue ribbon, don't you think?" I pranced my eleven-year-old body around the crowded kitchen, clutching the blouse to my chest, pretending to strut a fashion runway.

Her voice and look stopped me. "Janet, you don't think you're going to enter that blouse in the fair, do you?"

Startled, I stopped in mid-prance, gaping in astonishment. She quietly continued: "You have plenty of time to make another. That one's not completely your work. I fixed it for you so you wouldn't be discouraged. Would it be honest to enter it?" Once again, visions of myself with a blue ribbon denoting my excellence, shattered to disbelief. What was she talking about? Who would even know? Surely, she didn't mean I should start over.

One look at her unyielding expression as she opened the back door and headed for the orderly rows of her family-feeding garden, told me she meant just that; and there would be no more discussion. Again furious tears, again a slammed screen door, again the quiet refuge of my tree. But this time, my anger disguised shame. I knew she would not relent, no matter how much I cried and pleaded; and I knew she was right. Quietly, still hiccupping from useless sobs, I climbed down from my haven.

I slowly entered the garden, inched along a row of pepper plants covered with tiny green globes, met my mother's eyes, and offered my opener: "May I choose any fabric I want for the next blouse I make?"

The Changing Sound of Air

My thoughts buzzed, angry and mutinous: "I can't make it. I'm going to die at 8:00 in the morning, slumped over a giant rock, legs churning uselessly, granola bar uneaten. I'm not taking another step. I'm finished." I lurched to a stop and bent over, open-mouthed and drooling like an exhausted dog.

Friends had assured me that climbing a Colorado fourteener would be a thrilling experience, one that would change my life. I now realized, as my screeching lungs threatened to explode, that the promised change could be toting around an oxygen tank for the rest of my life.

My husband and I had started at dawn, carrying light packs with a minimum of emergency gear and walking briskly from the campground to the head of the trail we had chosen for our hike up Mt. Elbert near Leadville. The air pushed cool against my face; my steps stretched long and loose; my breathing flowed effortlessly—a silent, automatic companion. Feeling alive and invigorated, I flashed a grin at Joel. As we started the ascent, I began breathing through my mouth to accommodate my need for increased oxygen, smooth inhalations that tasted fresh.

The trail steepened. My breathing quickened and grew heavy, as though a doctor had told me to breathe deeply, again and again, while he listened through his stethoscope.

The trail drew up even more. The swoosh of my breath became a soft whistle on the inhale and a slight moan on the exhale. I slowed, became deliberate with my foot placement, wiped my face with my sleeve. Soon the path veered and revealed an incline ahead of at least eighty degrees—a zigzagging line of lightening. As I climbed it, the sun-warmed air began to sob in and out of my lungs, each gasp fighting its own passage. My eyes watered. A ground troll seemed to have latched onto my feet, determined I shouldn't pass. I promised myself that for every twenty steps I managed, I could rest. Step…huff…step…puff…step…huff.

An obstacle course blocked my way—large, sharp rocks requiring arduous steps up and over. Now my exchange of air sounded like a shrieking teakettle at full boil, my tortured lungs insisting that nothing in our sixty-three years of co-dependency had prepared them for this task. I considered discarding a tissue, thinking I would rather litter than carry the heavy item another step.

I tried not to look ahead, but I did. And I saw. Soon we would be walking a vertical line, straight into the sky, in danger of toppling over backward, bouncing from boulder to boulder, wiping out unwary hikers below. I fastened my eyes on the toes of my hiking boots, double-tied, oppressive burdens, not at all like walking on pillows as the outdoor gear catalogue had promised. I concentrated my will: one step, now another, one step, now another. My breathing bellowed and squawked like a mangled accordion, a disturbing noise that accompanied each step until it reached a manic crescendo devoid of any rhythm. The stream from my eyes blended with the sweat running from my brow and the mucus leaking from my nose. My feet were dead.

"Good work, Ma'am," a cheerful hiker encouraged as he glided down from the summit, "You've finished the approach and can start really climbing now. Great morning, isn't it?"

My lungs shattered. My vocabulary turned ugly. I took another step.

Hooked on Books

My life-long love affair with libraries and books began when Mom drove us along Lake Shore's gravel roads to the Spanish Fork library, which stood in an expanse of grass and trees on the small town's main street. We ran up fifteen steps and into the dimly lit building, where we scattered across the hardwood floors to our favorite sections like marbles dropped from a bag. After searching and sampling, we traveled home with our books, arguing over who had made the best selections.

When we were adults, I asked my youngest brother JL what he remembered about living in Spanish Fork after we moved there from Lake Shore. His response was immediate and specific: the library bulging with a treasure-trove of books he couldn't wait to read.

As a youngster, JL wrestled, ran, and roughhoused. A variety of startling noises burst from him for no apparent reason and at no particular time. He chortled with a whole-hearted, infectious laugh. Dirt found him. At the table, he displayed more enthusiasm than nicety. And yet, in contrast to his rowdy behaviors, this rambunctious, youngest brother caught the reading bug, early and permanently.

When he was six, JL joined a summer book club held in the children's section of the library. Every Wednesday, rookie readers assembled as a wriggling mass, sitting cross-legged on a faded rug, to listen to a story before being allowed to browse the crowded shelves. JL, well versed in body-blocking and evasive maneuvers from skirmishes at home with Blaine, excelled in the race to find the best picture books, though he already had his eye on the ragged collection of Oz books housed just beyond his reach.

Each week, he insisted that he be properly attired and on time for his literary soiree. Proper attire meant his homemade cowboy shirt tucked in straight—no wrinkles or sags—his pants pulled high, his belt buckled tight. On time meant when Blaine and he were dropped off early to play in the park, anxiety about being late would build in him as they threw one another off the merry-go-round until he erupted: "Don't you think we'd better go, Blaine? I think we're late. Don't you? We'd better go. Come on. Hurry." Then they'd stand on the front steps, first in line, twenty minutes early.

We lived on Canyon Road, three miles from the library, a long trek for six-year-old legs, no matter how sturdy and determined their owner. We had one car, a battered blue Plymouth, in which JL was taxied back and forth to his literary soiree. But on some Wednesdays, Dad worked days and had to drive, leaving the boys stranded. Blaine shrugged and went outside to throw clods at Barbara. JL became frantic; the highlight of his summer was in peril.

I shared his passion for reading: so, even though my primary need at sixteen was to avoid looking like a dork, I pumped him down the hill on our rusted-out, police-auction bicycle while he fussed loudly about my lack of speed making him late. During story time, I loitered in the back of the room, observing the restless horde, listening to their inane questions, and rethinking my desire to be a teacher.

Then, sweating and puffing, going out of my way to avoid the homes of friends, I conveyed him back up the hill as he jabbered about his selections: *Horton Hears a Who*, *A Fly Went By*, or *Henry Huggins*. And because he was so excited about reading and rereading his books, I didn't mind putting my social standing at risk to chauffeur him.

To this day, my favorite conversations with JL begin, "Hey, read any good books lately?"

Where Everybody Knows
Your Name

We wanted a reason to remain outdoors. Soft light, sandwiched between dusk and dark, flattered our aging neighborhood; cool air, swirling through cottonwood leaves and rogue hollyhocks, nudged away the heat of summer. "Janet," my husband suggested, "let's walk two blocks over to see how the remodeling is going."

We flip-flopped along old sidewalks, cracked and uplifted like ice floes, to our destination where we joined a small group of neighbors and dog-walkers in front of a modest home being transformed for its young family. Opinions flowed. We were happy the renovation didn't disturb the elderly trees hovering over the lot. We admired the skillful blending of the addition with the existing home and debated colors for the new siding. An elderly lady commented to her grinning husband, "You know, Ted, we could remodel if you'd quit buying snow machines." Eventually, all of us issued our stamp of approval to the home's new look and sauntered away.

Welcome to Craig, where neighbors notice.

The first definition for neighbor in my battered 1964 student-edition dictionary is *a person who lives near another.* The broader, second definition—*fellow man, as in love your fellow man*—is a better fit for

Craig, because it allows us to monitor more people.

I decided I wanted to grow old in this inquisitive community when one of its watchful members gave my father a needed assist. My dad, ninety, visited Joel and me in 1999. One morning we went to work before Dad got out of bed, so I left breakfast food for him on the counter. The phone rang as I was leaving, and I took time to jot directions to a location where I had a meeting that evening.

When Dad wandered into the kitchen, awake and hungry, he overlooked the food, but saw my scribbled directions sitting on top of the microwave. "Hmm," he thought, "Janet must think I'd like breakfast at this place."

He donned his straw cowboy hat and left, turning west instead of east at the end of our driveway, so he didn't end up in a residential area looking for a non-existent restaurant. Instead, miraculously, my directions, "One block, turn left, two blocks, turn right, straight ahead, white siding," led him to a small cafe.

Full of food and high spirits, Dad decided to take a stroll around town on his way home. Twenty minutes later, he came to a park. Realizing he didn't know where he was, he decided a nap might be helpful; so he snoozed on the grass with his hat shading his face for some time, and then sat up. The rest cure had failed. He was still lost. He then felt an elderly parent's common concern—fear that he'd be a bother to his busy child.

Later that morning, I received a call from a mail carrier: "Mrs. Sheridan, I just wanted to tell you that walking my route earlier today, I noticed an elderly gentleman sitting on the grass in the Breeze Park and went to see if he needed help. He told me he was visiting his daughter, Janet Sheridan, went out for a walk, couldn't find his way back, and would like to get home on his own without bothering her. So I directed him to your house and watched until he turned into the right place. Hope that's OK."

Without hesitating, knowing it was against regulations for a post-office employee to reveal the address of a resident, taking in the age and pride of the gentleman before him, this kind person made a Craig decision. Small towns, peopled with neighbors who know you, are to be prized, praised, and lived in for a long time.

Part 3 Fall

The transformation of seasons begins in a late-August instant when a cool breeze sneaks into town, mingles with the tired air of summer, and brushes by startled faces. AA single leaf of fiery red peeks from a green hedge, and bold orange banners appear on downtown businesses to welcome hunters to Craig, "Elk Hunting Capital of the World."

A spreading quilt of golden terrain and shorter days arguing with a standoffish sun mark our increasing distance from summer; and excited children abandon their shorts and sandals to dress in back-to-school clothes and bounce around town in swarming buses.

We gaze at low-flying geese silhouetted against mountains of aspen yellow and catch the distant clamor of Friday night football games. When we awaken in the early morning hours to pull blankets up around our shoulders, we wonder which fall day will deliver our first dusting of snow.

A Known World

Nothing compares to the first day of school for stomach-fluttering excitement: new teachers, different classmates, and unmarked report cards. As a child, I anticipated endless summers. Then, as quickly as seeds can be blown from a dandelion, the first day of school arrived; and, contrary to our sleepy-headed natures, my siblings and I appeared at the bus stop early and completely groomed. We felt excitement more than anxiety, because at Lake Shore Elementary, we entered a known world.

We knew what time the bus doors would pop open at our stop, which dim-witted boys would try to trip us in the aisle, and where long-standing tradition would allow us to sit: kindergarten babies and first graders in the front, sophisticated sixth graders in the back, and the undistinguished masses muddled in between. We knew the bus driver—Schroeder of grease-begrimed coveralls and booming voice— and his rule: if anyone displeased him in any way, he would stop the bus and the offenders would walk.

From kindergarten through sixth grade, I went to school with the same twenty children. We knew each other as well as we knew the outline of the princess on top of Mt. Timpanogas who kept watch over our school. My classmates and I ran in and out of one another's houses, squabbled with each other's siblings, and obeyed any parent without question. Many of us attended the same family reunions. We could predict who would be chosen first for kickball, who would win the spelling bees, and who would lie during show and tell. Had our new teachers shown interest, we could have reported on one other's church attendance and the number of children, horses, and dogs in each family.

We had another advantage as well: When the bell rang to start the first day, we faced a teacher whose eccentricities our siblings had described in detail. We were warned in advance about chalk throwers, hard graders, saliva sprayers, homework assigners, and burpers.

From experience, we knew the grandmotherly cooks would serve us chili and fresh-baked cinnamon rolls every Friday, and that the principal would ignore playground fights unless they resulted in bloody noses or broken glasses. We expected the annual warning from the office that no more rubber balls would be issued if we kept kicking them on top of the school.

The elderly custodian who let us pull the rope that rang the tower bell made each one of us believe he liked us best. Year in and year out, we giggled at his standard reply when we thanked him for handing us our milk, "You're Welshman—if you don't marry a Danishman."

As a group, we dreaded the nightmare day when the school halls smelled of alcohol and we were marched to the cafeteria for our shots. We knew which classmates would faint, which would claim they didn't feel a thing, and which boys would threaten to hit our sore shoulders.

And always, day in and day out in our small redbrick school, we were certain that if we didn't behave, our parents would deal with us more severely than the principal.

My rural classmates and I went to school in a simpler time and place. We were secure in the predictability of our days: safe among our knowns.

Bossy Janet

When young, I admired my mother's decisive nature: "Janet," she'd say as I sprawled on the couch rereading *Little Women*, "you need to learn how to change Blaine's diaper. Come here. And quit wrinkling your nose."

She ordered me to brush my teeth and lace my shoes. She decided my book-besotted mind needed the challenge of clarinet lessons. At a church social, she insisted I dance with Justin Clinton, a runty mouth-breather who rested his chin on my hipbone. She told me to adopt a hobby: perhaps a collection. Then, when I suggested I could collect ice cream—trying to eat and list 100 different flavors in a year—she replied, "Oh, good grief, Janet, no!"

I began to imitate Mom's take-charge behavior. I confiscated the tube of toothpaste Ruthie Tuckett was snacking on during Sunday school. I explained Betty Anderson had not turned a correct cartwheel because her legs were bent like a rolling potato bug. I stepped out of my role as Queen Lily in the fourth-grade play and impressed the audience by correcting the mistakes of my fellow actors: "The word is chocolate, Ronald, not chonklate, and Bruce, stop teetering on your throne. Sit still!" I told my sister Barbara that her bangs looked ugly and fixed them with pinking shears. Before we went to church the next day, Mom painted the bald spot on Barbara's head with brown shoe polish.

Then one hot September day, I wandered into the sticky kitchen where Mom was bottling peaches. I had an important question: how should I describe myself to my pen pal? Imagine my dismay when the woman I admired and imitated told me to write that I was tall, with mostly uncombed hair, and bossy—very bossy. I didn't mind the uncombed part; it was true. But bossy? My jaw bounced, fell to my chest, and stayed unhinged for days. A strangled sound escaped me.

Without seeming to notice my need for artificial respiration, Mom said I could lose friends if I continued telling everyone what to do all the time, acting like the boss of the world. At that indignity, my eyes bulged; my face flashed hot; and I shrieked like a peacock chasing a peahen, "What do you mean? *You're* always telling *me* what to do."

Mom tapped the handle of a table knife on the lids of some cooled jars to check their seal, then answered: "Janet, helping your child improve and mature is being a mother. Correcting friends for their lack of perfection is being rude. I'm a parent. You're bossy."

Tears worked their way down my face. In a room silent except for my sobs, Mom used her dishtowel to wipe the edges of jars she had filled and continued: "You can't say everything that pops into your head. How would Mr. Bigelow feel if I told him he shouldn't sing because his voice makes babies and dogs howl? What would Mrs. Beck think if I said her habit of taking a second helping of dessert could make her bottom as big as a washtub?"

A giggle spluttered through my sobs; Mom smiled, "You know I would never say those things. I would offend people, and they would begin to avoid me. You need to think about how your words make others feel, Janet."

As she pulled a rack of sterilized jars from a steaming pot of water, I skulked away, muttering.

Despite my hurt feelings, I remembered the words my mother delivered in a steamy kitchen as she canned peaches. So now, when I consider asking a cousin to quit using "you know" as a comma when she talks, I close my mouth—and thank my mother.

Preferred Seating

Folks seem to stress over seating arrangements as much as they do over telemarketers who call during dinner, deer that eat begonias, and dentists who say, "Oh-oh." In buses and planes, family vans, crowded meetings, and office break rooms, people fuss about where they sit.

When my family gathered at the dinner table, Dad and Mom anchored each end. The rest of us occupied the middle ground on a first-come first-served basis. The punishment for fighting at the table was banishment; and we did love our food, so our battles over preferred accommodations were sneaky, delivered and suffered in silence—an elbow here, a straight-arm there, a hip strategically placed to block access. Our parents, to preserve their sanity, mostly ignored our muffled thuds and stifled moans.

They imposed stricter rules when we wedged into our plucky Plymouth: Mom, Dad, and babies or toddlers occupied the front seat. The rest squashed into the back with the oldest two granted the privilege of sitting by the windows—which is why the youngest prayed nightly for those older to find happiness in an early marriage. I hated sitting by Carolyn. She enforced a no-touching rule with pinches and hissed threats if any part of my body nudged hers.

I'm convinced that most adults emerged from childhood with painful memories of such maneuverings and a fixation about seating.

About six weeks into my first year of teaching, I'd developed a sense of pacing, which enabled me to take an actual lunch break, rather than gulping Twinkies at my desk as I tried to get ready for thirty students to return in thirty-five minutes for three more hours. So the next day, I approached the teachers' lounge carrying my tuna sandwich. Cigarette smoke rolled from the vent in the door, showing me the way, and friendly voices greeted me as I walked through the stale haze to the end of the table and sat on a plastic chair sporting a cushion with a crocheted cover.

Chatter stopped. A communal intake of breath made the blinds chatter. Alarmed, I looked up to see Mrs. Devlin materialize through the gray cloud. She carried a lipstick-smeared coffee cup, eyed me coldly through the smoke of the cigarette that dangled from the corner of her scarlet mouth, and rasped one word: "Move."

I did.

As a consultant, whenever I taught a series of workshops, unofficial seating charts were evident by the second session: those three had to sit together; that one needed the seat nearest the door; those six couldn't be budged from the back; those two always pulled their chairs away from the table to block the aisle; and I could have stretched out and snoozed on the vacant seats in the front row.

If a creative custodian arranged the chairs and tables in a different pattern, confusion reigned until the participants busily dragged a chair here or a table there and re-established their comfort zones.

The same sort of territorialism exists on airplanes. Though a few kind souls will volunteer to switch seats so a family won't be separated, most fliers lock their jaws, clamp onto their arm rests, and avoid eye contact with the pleading party.

Couples also adopt seating patterns. In a restaurant, Joel insists on having the seat with the most expansive view of the other diners. In his hometown, where people haven't forgotten, I could understand his need to protect his back. But in Denver? As a result of his obsession, I dine with a view of the bathroom door, the steamy kitchen, or a wall adorned with artificial flowers.

At least he doesn't enforce a no-touch rule.

Thoughts Inspired by Our September Anniversary

I'm often surprised by the odd habits of others: Some bake brownies without walnuts. Why do they bother? Some stay up beyond 9:00. How do they do that? Some open their presents on Christmas Eve. What do they do the next morning? In college, it boggled my mind when my roommates postponed studying for a test until the evening before and then pulled an all-nighter. I shook my well-rested head in disbelief as they stumbled into class, bleary-eyed and confused.

My mom and dad ate pickled pigs feet and liver. I don't.

My uncle wrote a weekly column for his local paper. Each week he sat in front of his typewriter the day before the column was due and waited for inspiration. When I picture him—sitting, waiting, clock ticking, deadline looming—I fight hysteria. I don't know how he found the time to debate using *a* instead of *the* in the third sentence of the fifth paragraph of the ninth revision.

My sister collects nothing: no quilts, snow globes, miniature spoons, matchbooks, or tractors. I think she's strange.

The man I married eleven years ago has his peculiarities as well, one of them being his viewing habits. When we watch TV, I like to tune into something we know we like and watch it. He prefers to pound on the remote to see if there's something better on another channel. Even after we agree on what to watch, he surfs other channels during commercials. By the time he finds his way back to the program we chose, we've missed a pivotal part of the show and watch the rest in a state of confusion.

When I watch a movie on TV, I pay attention to the mood-establishing opening credits. When Joel watches with me, he employs his thumb—spoon-shaped from constant use—to zoom by the first three minutes; and then I whine. It's a win-win situation: he gets to play telegraph operator on the remote, and I enjoy a pity party.

Another bone of contention we chew on is the degree of lighting necessary for happy living. As darkness falls, I busy myself drawing blinds and switching on lights and lamps. If I don't watch carefully, Joel wanders in and carries on a diverting conversation while turning off the lamps and dimming the lights.

Even the kitchen where I chop, sauté, and simmer his dinner is too bright for him. If I drop my guard, he extinguishes the overhead lighting, leaving only the glow of the under-counter lights to illuminate my cooking. It's difficult to chop vegetables when I can't distinguish my thumb from a parsnip; and sometimes, when bending low to check on the soup's simmer, I blister my nose.

My husband believes the best defense is a good offense, so when he senses my irritation with his choice of lighting, he asks, "Why do you have to have it so bright all the time? The house looks better in low light."

He could be commenting on my housekeeping, but I prefer to think not.

We also have our smaller issues: I put things away. He likes tools, clothes and crackers left where he won't forget he has them. I sigh when he questions my organization. He grits his teeth when I respond to a preference he mentions—"I like the chair better in front of the window"—with a dismissive, "I know you do, Joel."

Despite these differences, most of the time we accept one another's oddities as minor nuisances, insignificant when compared to the many important values we share and the many ways we like each other.

But the next time we go to a movie, and he interrupts an intense scene to ask what other roles the lead actor has played, I plan to insist on a fair share of the popcorn. That'll show him.

Uncle Bud

Bob, Carolyn, and I abandoned the leaf fight we waged beneath shedding cottonwood trees and ran to the front lawn to watch the regal progress of Uncle Bud's Cadillac. It floated along our bumpy lane, raising a celebratory plume of dust like an exclamation point. Mom joined us, wiping her hands on her apron and wearing a cautious expression, though a smile flickered across her face. "Go tell your father Bud's here," she instructed.

We knew how pleased Dad would be to see his younger brother, his full brother, in a family peopled with the offspring of a disliked stepfather. A bond existed between Dad and Bud, a commitment forged in the face of their punitive stepfather, erratic mother, and absent father.

The smell of leather seats and heavy perfume mingled with Uncle Bud's laugh as he exited his Caddy, a new woman in tow. I craned my neck to take in the hugeness of this uncle who made my 6'2" father look puny. A black shirt and white tie struggled to constrain his bulging chest and thick neck. A black straw hat with a red band tilted to the back of his head and an ivory toothpick clung to the corner of his mouth as he laughed at our excitement. I liked his laugh. It boomed from his dented face, flowed from openhearted happiness, and showed his gold tooth to advantage.

Like my father, Uncle Bud worked in a steel plant. But their lives diverged when not on the job. While Dad cared for a small farm and a large family, Uncle Bud pursued booze, brawls, and women. He devoted energy and skill to his favored pastimes and was rewarded with court appearances, a raised-eyebrows reputation, and six wives. According to Dad, Bud's first wife Maudie caused his wild ways: she broke his heart when he returned from World War II by revealing she loved another. Maudie's perfidy sent Uncle Bud careening from bar to bar: meeting, marrying, and divorcing women willing to drink with a cheerful man who always sobered up in time for his shift and was generous with his paycheck.

On this day of autumn exuberance, Uncle Bud had driven to Lake Shore to introduce us to wife number seven, a large woman with a southern accent, prim lacquered mouth, expansive bosom, and startling red-orange hair. She smiled shyly, clutched a leopard-print purse to her tummy, and murmured, "Pleased to meet y'all." Later, Uncle Bud told Dad that he met our new aunt under a pool table during a drunken fight and decided to marry her on the spot because she was "real pretty passed out under there."

My siblings and I loved this uncle: his good nature, his generosity, his ability to surprise laughter from my mom. But we knew he didn't fit, wasn't comfortable, in our world. When I was older, I realized that in Dad's family—a family of miners, fighters and drinkers; of divorce, domestic disputes, and desertion—Bud's life was the norm. I also understood that Dad—who stayed sober, loved his family, and proved himself by outworking other men rather than fighting them—didn't fit, felt uncomfortable, around those who raised him.

But Dad and Bud did fit, were comfortable, in each other's hearts.

My uncle died a terrible death, labeled an industrial accident, slipping on a skywalk, sliding beneath a guardrail, plunging into a red-hot river of molten slag. Suicide was whispered, but we could never reconcile that rumor with the man we knew. His brother's death diminished my father. He lost his song, abandoned his whistle, and mourned.

The Wonder of Words Well Chosen

During sharing time, we hitched our chairs forward, drawing closer to the warmth that radiated from Mrs. Thomas. We offered her our feelings and unfledged thoughts, knowing she would handle them as carefully as she did the geraniums growing on the windowsill. She carried a lacy white handkerchief tucked into her sleeve, a faint scent of lavender, and the habit of looking into our eyes as though we mattered. She gentled us with her quiet, kind core. We loved her. But we didn't give her our affection readily. For some of us, it took at least twenty minutes.

On the first day of fourth grade in 1951, dressed in stiff jeans and plaid shirts or homemade dresses trimmed with rickrack, we eyed our new teacher. Together we had survived an unforgiving disciplinarian in first grade, a pregnant missus belching and munching crackers in second, and Mrs. Beale, who couldn't control her saliva, in third. All had taught us adequately; none had captured our hearts. So far, this one didn't look promising either.

Mrs. Thomas resembled our soft-bodied grandmothers in their Sunday best: sturdy dresses, limited adornment, sensible shoes. Face powder settled in the wrinkles around her eyes, and pin curls imposed a rigid structure on her hair. When she walked the rows of wooden desks, handing out papers for us to do while she worked with small groups at the reading circle, I could hear her hose rubbing.

She called my name with the second group. Five minutes later I capitulated. I don't know how she won the hearts of my classmates, but I remember in detail how she captured mine. I entered the circle of short, wooden chairs with confidence. Reading was my thing. I planned to show this new teacher what a winner looks like. I plopped into a small seat and shifted uncomfortably, moving my long legs about, trying to decide where to put them. After three years of schooling, I associated uneasy seating with reading group. Tall for my age, I thought it normal to read with my chin between my knees, hunched like a buzzard among meadowlarks.

I experimented with a wide-legged sprawl, pushing the skirt of my dress between my legs so no one could see my new panties, decorated with flowers and the word Monday, so I'd know when to wear them. Next, I attempted to corkscrew one leg three times around the other. I was limbering up my ankles, thinking I could force both legs backward beneath the chair, when I heard a murmured, "Janet," and met the twinkling eyes of Mrs. Thomas. She was smiling at me like Mom did when I amused her without knowing how. "Janet, let's move this chair into the group for you. I think it will be a better fit your long, elegant legs."

Oh, my goodness—long, elegant legs! I knew how they looked: their awkward length was adorned with scabby knees, clawed mosquito bites, and yellow bruises from falling off the family cow. But the wonder of her words made me smile. She didn't say, "My, you're a big one. Maybe if you sit here, you'll quit scrabbling around like a crab looking for shelter." Instead, her words made me feel beautiful. I was smitten, captured by a sensitive teacher who noticed my discomfort and chose her words with care.

Twelve years later, I stood outside a doorway, listening to excited voices flowing from within. I took a deep breath, whispered, "Stay with me today, Mrs. Thomas; help me notice the beauty of each," and entered my classroom as a first-year teacher.

Moments With My Mother

My earliest memory is of the comfort my mother gave me when I awoke in darkness to a crescendo of crickets as fever surged through my body. Pain entangled my thoughts; mussed bedding trapped my limbs. I heard whimpers, but didn't know who was crying. A familiar presence appeared at my bedside, palmed hair from my forehead, freed me from sodden sheets. I was offered sips of warm liquid, then soothed until I found sleep.

When I was thirteen, I formed another vivid memory of my mother when we were asked to be the featured speakers at a Dear to My Heart Night for the mothers and daughters of our church. I don't remember working on my tribute to Mom, or what I said, but I do remember fussing endlessly with my bangs, gluing them in place with Brylcreem and hair spray, more concerned with my appearance than my words.

I still have a hand-written copy of Mom's speech. She began with startling news: "Janet, from the moment I first held your warm, perfect body in my arms and gloated over your dark, curly ducktails—I finally had a baby with hair—you've been a source of joy and delight to me and the entire family."

The entire family? Even Bob? Did they get to vote?

Later in her speech, another surprise: "I enjoy leaving your younger sister and brothers in your care. I know that even if the dishes are sketchily done and the furniture pushed awry, the little ones will be well cared for and have fun as you create games and stories for them. You'd be a good teacher, Janet." With those words, she directed me toward my future.

Mom made my heart soar that night; then, driving home, she returned me to earth: "Janet, we have to do something about those shaggy bangs stuck to your nose. As soon as we get home, I'm cutting them. You look like a greasy Shetland pony." She laughed at her description of my unshorn appearance, and I had to join her.

When Mom was seventy-seven, I spent a week with her in early October. Most of the time we talked about anything that popped into our heads, worked on projects, and enjoyed Dad's antics. Other times, I sat with a book in my lap and watched her sleep in a recliner; her hands unusually idle in the middle of the day. Soft window light bathed her lined face, and her breath seemed slow and faint.

Not wanting to worry her children, she admitted she'd had some heart problems, but said her medicine and pacemaker helped. As I sat with her, watching her drift in and out of sleep, I refused to recognize the truth.

She died seven months later. With time, I recovered from the emotional turmoil of her death, funeral, and burial—a poignant week I moved through with my father and siblings, united in grief and love. Then the long-term ache of her absence began.

Two years after her funeral, I absentmindedly drove a Carson City street of golden leaves let fall by tired trees. My neck tight with stress, I worried personal choices, professional puzzles, a life littered with busy-ness. Turning a corner, I glimpsed a woman on the sidewalk who reminded me of myself: face touched by age, long flowing skirt, and heels of a practical height. Her head inclined, she walked in slow stages toward a nursing home, tenderly holding the frail arm of a stooped sparse-haired woman. Both were slender and tall with identical smiles. As I watched, they paused and commented above a bed of purple asters.

Without warning, my heart collapsed like a butterfly caught in a net, and I mourned: I never walked my mother through her decline; I lived far away, thought I'd have time; others were there. And she died so quickly.

I grieved because there would be no more memories.

Sous Chef Wanted

Late October: nearly time for the parade of treats and feasts that lasts until we've celebrated the New Year. When I think of the cleaning and cooking required by our holiday festivities— scouring sinks, dusting furniture, chopping onions, carving turkey—I sigh, feel faint, get teary-eyed.

My aversion to cleaning is well documented; my relationship with cooking is more ambivalent: when I have plenty of time and all the ingredients, it's fun; but when the cream sauce refuses to thicken and the bread dough won't rise, it's miserable. My first solo cooking adventure involved tapioca pudding and disaster. Probably because I attempted to read the funnies, badger Barbara, and cook at the same time, I reversed the measurements for sugar and salt, using a pinch of the first and a half-cup of the second. When I served it for Sunday dinner, my siblings gagged, clutched their throats, and went into death throes. Dad tried to stop my tears by eating the lumpy brine, saying he worked in the heat all day and his body needed lots of salt. One spoonful seemed to take care of his deficit.

As a result of my many cooking snafus, I envy the calmness and skill of TV chefs; but I wonder what happens when they cook at home, unassisted by staff and undistracted by family. Do they pour excess water off half-cooked rice, strain lumps out of gravy, and flap a hand towel at their shrieking smoke detector every time they open their ovens? I watch chefs in spotless TV kitchens and think I could talk and cook simultaneously, wearing a smile and spotless clothes, if I had a team to trim the fat, toast the nuts, and peel the shrimp.

I'd like an assistant who could produce a uniform chop, dice, or mince on any vegetable or fruit—a task that baffles me. My chopping method is to flail away at a butternut squash with a knife too dull on a board too small until I can't stand it anymore and decide massive, irregular chunks will suffice.

I want an assembler who would study my recipes and find all the ingredients I tucked away absentmindedly after shopping. If I'd forgotten the rhubarb for the rhubarb pie, the assembler could run to the store while I pressed my apron. This detail-oriented person could also pre-measure all ingredients—flour, mayonnaise, honey—and put them into little glass bowls lined up in the order needed. Then I could tell jokes as I added ingredients to my mixing bowl without looking, just like on TV.

My next hire would be a pots, utensils, and tableware expert who would possess perfect depth perception and proportion discernment in order to gather casseroles, loaf pans, and skillets of the correct size and shape. This helper would also select appropriate serving dishes—the first time. Too often, I pour a chocolate-caramel pudding into a lovely bowl only to discover it looks like an insignificant puddle at the bottom of the Grand Canyon. I could use the time saved by my selector to polish my French accent.

I'd have a timer on my staff to remember small details that elude me: preheating the skillet so added ingredients sizzle deliciously rather than lying in a cold, sodden lump, or watching anything I attempt to broil so I wouldn't have to scrape off blackened bits before serving it. The timer would turn on the oven so it's ready when I slide in the pumpkin pie and turn it off when the pie is done—no more staring in sleepy-eyed amazement at an oven left on all night.

Finally, a nagger would come in handy to remind me to never again attempt homemade candy. Never.

No wonder I'm exhausted by the time I've prepared a meal. I've done the work of six.

Don't Invite Me to Your Costume Party

I remember receiving an invitation to an adult costume party where guests were expected to dress as their worst nightmare. I broke out in hives. Such a party *is* my worst nightmare.

My phobia began with my first-grade teacher, Mrs. Hathaway, who dressed up for our community Halloween party as a shepherd. She wore a brown bathrobe, pulled its hood over her head, and carried a bamboo fishing pole as her staff. It was probably the best she could do after rushing home to spend hours grading our papers, as we assumed she did on a daily basis.

When garbing herself, Mrs. Halliday didn't realize that Ginny Madison and I had recently discovered the specter of death in a battered encyclopedia in the school library. Though we couldn't read the text, we fell into open-mouthed horror at the sketches of a gaunt, skull-headed creature wearing a hooded robe and carrying a scythe as it presided over a variety of anguished deaths. As our tall, costumed teacher approached us in the gym, Ginny and I were struck by her resemblance to the ghoulish creature in the encyclopedia. We howled and clung to the legs of our embarrassed and puzzled mothers.

The transformation of my teacher into the grim reaper put a

damper on my relationship with dress-up, but I had to wear costumes. That's what children do on Halloween.

In second grade, Mom tried to lighten the mood by concocting a clown costume for me. As part of the get-up, I wore pants from my brother's outgrown pajamas, gathered and ruffled at the ankle and safety-pinned at the waist for fit. All went well at the party until, after repeated visits to the homemade root beer stand, I went to the restroom. I could not squeeze the safety pin, fat with folds of fabric, tight enough to release it. I spent several long minutes—jiggling up and down, working on the pin, muttering Dad's favorite words—before the inevitable happened. For the rest of the night, I viciously elbowed friends who asked why I was wearing my coat.

In fourth grade, our teacher announced a contest to see whose costumes camouflaged them so well their fellow students wouldn't recognize them. I dressed as a witch, because wearing a mask I made from a paper sack, a wig Mom made from a mop dyed black, and Aunt Mary's mothball-smelling, black-velvet prom dress stuffed with pillows, guaranteed a win. Instead, I was the first person eliminated. I had forgotten I was a head taller than all of my classmates.

Things didn't improve in fifth grade. I decided to take advantage of my height and wear a costume no one else could duplicate. I would go as a tree, a towering tree, graced by fall foliage. Mom accepted the challenge. She used gunnysacks to create a loose-fitting trunk to wear over my body. She cut a knothole opening for my face and sewed a tipsy fabric owl on top of my head. My arms served as branches. I spent an evening cutting leaves from construction paper and stapling them to my gunnysack sleeves.

When it was time for the costume parade, I stood tall and waved my branches about, hooting like an owl, hoping to win. To my jump-up-and-down joy, I did; but I paid for my victory the rest of the evening: two sixth-grade hoodlums, Nicky Cooper and Bernie White, followed me everywhere I went, towing a first-grader dressed as a dachshund and commanding, "Hey, Davey, go pee on that tree."

To this day, I don't do well with costumes. I admire those who do—but I will not be joining them.

Schroeder's Auto Repair

My dad's birthday was two weeks after mine. We shared the birth month of November and the answer to Mom's question about what kind of cake we wanted for our celebratory dinners: raisin cake with caramel frosting. When I think of my dad, I tend to recall the ordinary—the life he led day to day—more than the momentous.

I remember the many times he took us to Schroeder's, despite the lack of ready cash. Screen door slamming, tall, work-slim body striding through the yard, he yelled to any of his children within hearing, "If you want to go with me, climb aboard. I'm on my way."

Word spread: "He might stop at Schroeder's." Deserting chores, we scrambled into our bedraggled jeep, elbowing for front-seat position. Singing about taking some lady named Kathleen home again, Dad gunned the engine and shot away, paying no mind to his children still in mid-scramble.

A fast five miles of irrigated farmland flashed by, dotted by an occasional house hunched beneath massive outbuildings. The finger-smeared windows through which we peered softened the countryside and gentled its farmyard clutter. Dad, more interested in his vibrato than our battles, bounced the jeep along rough roads in tempo to his tune, until, gravel flying, he executed his usual abrupt stop. "Whoa there, old boy, whoa there," he shouted to our great amusement as he flamboyantly pulled back on the wheel and stomped on the brakes at Schroeder's Auto Repair.

The single, rusted-out gas pump reflecting long departed prices held no allure for us; nor did the garage's shadowed interior with its thick air that smelled of rubber and oil. We didn't stop to examine Schroeder's grease-begrimed tools or the fly-spotted glass case holding PayDay bars, Juicy Fruit gum, and hide-a-key containers. Instead, clutching unfamiliar dimes Dad distributed from a near-empty wallet—an act our money-worried mother wouldn't approve—we ran to the rectangular soda machine sitting like a dusty treasure chest in a far corner, burbling moistly to itself.

While Dad discussed man things—lay-offs, unemployment checks, failed crops—with big-voiced, thoroughly dirty Schroeder, we circled the red machine and argued best flavors: orange and strawberry being top contenders. Decisions made, we clinked our dimes into the coin slot. The machine's scratched red lid sighed reluctantly as we lifted it, exhaling cold air that washed over our peering faces.

Inside the rectangular chest, icy water bathed cold bottles that we slowly worked along notched metal rows until we could each lift our choice clear, remove its crimped cap with the built-in opener, and take the first sweetly stinging swallow. Carolyn, a teenager, assumed a pose of nonchalance and sophistication, drinking as though it was almost more than she could manage. Bob threw his head back and drank like the rowdy boy he was, pausing only to burp. I sipped, savoring and saving. Barbara, who had yet to grasp the science of swallowing, let orange liquid flow down her throat in an uninterrupted stream, plugging it with her tongue when she needed to breathe.

As we happily enjoyed our rare treat, Dad looked over at us and grinned. If the total of a man is made of small acts, our father was a giant.

Wanna Hickey

Each November 9th, as I enjoy an increasingly restrained celebration of the years I've attained, I'm reminded of an often overlooked event that happens at birth: the naming of innocent, trusting newborns who have no say in the matter.

How many times have you heard, "You'll never believe this, but in college I knew a girl named Wanna Hickey, hah, hah, hah. Get it?" Such statements are natural conversation starters; everyone in the room can participate, sharing hilarious names bestowed on precious babes— April Schauer, Walter Melon, Willie Leak.

As laughter abounds, I think about the tyke burdened with such a label for life, or until old enough to petition the courts for a name change. I had a friend named Betty Crocker who tired of being called Cake Mix and started the process of changing her name the day she turned eighteen. I'm glad my parents didn't welcomed me into the Bray clan by naming me Verda.

And what is this thing we have about bestowing nicknames on one another, our possessions, and ourselves? I resist this temptation. I don't rename my loved ones, my car, my toothbrush, or my body parts. I remember letting others clamor for the privilege of christening family pets, and I identified my dolls by descriptive phrases: baby doll, bald doll, armless doll, peeing doll. And because I didn't have children, I never had to decide which ancestral name would burden my offspring.

Perhaps my reluctance to name things arose from my disappointment with my given name. My parents did the best they could, but they had other things on their minds. Dad had started a new job after our move from California to Utah; three other children needed attention; and Mom's bed in the hall of the crowded Cottonwood Maternity Home was infested with bedbugs. She was preoccupied, unable to settle on a name, so Dad found it. Driving home after my birth, he caught sight of a name in red neon letters atop a shabby diner: Janet's Hamburgers. He admired the way it looked, spelled out in cursive, flashing boldly in the night, and thought it would be a beautiful name for his baby girl. He once told me he wanted to be true to the source and name me Janet Hamburger, but Mom refused. I think he was joking.

So I became Janet no-middle-name Bray. Mom, like her sisters, didn't have a middle name and didn't bestow one on any of her daughters. I never knew why.

In third grade, I asked my mother if I could switch names with my younger sister who was five and would never know the difference. I thought Barbara sounded more melodious than Janet. Listening to Mom read aloud from *One Hundred and One Famous Poems* must have developed my poetic sensitivities. It seemed obvious to me that Barbara Bray lilted. Janet Bray clanked. Barbara evoked images of tinkling laughter, bonbons, and small feet; Janet suggested boiled potatoes and sinus problems.

My name handicapped me. No one would expect Janet Bray to excel. Someone with such an unadorned name would never out-cute Shirley Temple or ride a rhinoceros. No. Those honors would go to Kelsey Cornaby or Annetta Anderson, Johanna Henderson, Lydia Lindstrom, or Roxie Throckmorton, girls with multi-syllabic, musical names: names that danced lightly on the tongue, sang. Meanwhile, Janet Bray would be stuck wearing hand-me-downs, fighting for a window seat, and catching pink eye—all because her name thumped through the airwaves like a hippo missing an appendage.

In sixth grade, my displeasure with Janet led to a monumental mistake. I informed my classmates that my name was French, properly pronounced Jah-nee, rhymes with nay, and they should start pronouncing it correctly. They seemed impressed until Frank Underwood challenged me: "Oh, yeah, how do you say your last name then?"

That's when I blundered. I haughtily replied, "It's not Bray, but Brah, rhymes with ah: Jahnee Brah."

With those words, I gave myself a nickname that caused unending amusement for everyone but me: for the rest of the year, I was called Maidenform.

I haven't named anything since.

No Surprises, Please

When I hear about surprise birthday parties, I break out in hives. I'm alarmed by the surprise, not the party. I like celebrating important events with friends and family members. But what's to enjoy about normally dignified people yelling "Surprise!" and leaping from drapes and houseplants while I stand agape, wishing I'd brushed my teeth?

When surprised, I'd like to respond with a ladylike exclamation of astonishment and glee, trilling, "Thank you. Oh, thank you so much!" I'd then like to work my way around the room, hugging and cooing, with appreciative tears making my eyes glisten charmingly. But I can't. Instead, I squeak and squeal and turn redder than Rudolph's nose.

The only thing worse than being ambushed by a group of shouting party animals is knowing their plan in advance. This happened to me on my thirtieth birthday when coworkers arranged a surprise party for me at a local restaurant. As a friend left work, she poked her head into my room and called, "Bye, Janet. See you tonight at the Mint!" Her horrified expression as she realized what she'd said aroused my suspicions, and her attempted cover-up verified them: "No! Wait! I mean... see you soon. Like tomorrow! For a minute!!" I went home, stood before a mirror, and tried to act surprised.

I'm no Meryl Streep.

I think my dislike of unexpected parties started when I was in first grade. My reading group read a Dick-and-Jane story in which Mother, Father, Dick, and Baby Sally surprised Jane by hiding her birthday presents. They then cheered, laughed lovingly, and gave clues—Spot barking along merrily—while clever Jane found her presents, each and every one. That night, I mentioned the story to my family at dinner.

A few weeks later on my birthday, I blearily entered the kitchen, trailing school clothes to pull on in front of the heater. Suddenly, annoying cries of "Surprise!" and "We hid your presents; you have to find them!!" assailed my fogged brain. For several minutes I dutifully wandered around in a confused stupor, finding nothing, as my family indulged in merriment devoid of helpful hints. I burst into tears and screeched that I hated them. How gracious.

The most disappointing consequence of surprise parties is that the individual being honored can't look forward to the celebration. Anticipation can be the best part of an experience: a Caribbean cruise, a new haircut, the arrival of a sweater ordered online. As we happily await these events, we picture perfection, not flies in the ointment. Then seasickness confines us to our cabin on captain's night; the new sweater verifies our weight gain, and the asymmetrical haircut makes us look strangely lop-sided.

A few year's ago, Joel's large family planned a surprise party for a beloved aunt's eightieth birthday. Folks assembled from near and far in a lodge at an Illinois state park to pay tribute to Aunt Renee, a dynamic lady with soft white hair and a cascading laugh that felt like a reward. We parked in a distant lot, corralled rambunctious children in the lobby, and checked the time compulsively. Finally, she entered, arm-in-arm with the niece who lured her there for lunch. "Surprise!" forty voices boomed.

We thought we'd killed her. She gasped, faltered, clutched her chest, and had to sit down. Several minutes passed before she regained her equanimity.

Later, she asked, "Why didn't you tell me you were going to have a party for my birthday, and everyone was coming? I could have anticipated it for weeks: planning what to wear, getting my hair done, and looking forward to seeing everybody."

After that experience, Joel and I vowed we'd never take part in planning a surprise party for one another. We don't want to make our exit gasping and flapping in a balloon-decorated room full of loved ones wearing party hats.

Pumpkin Pie and Aunt Mary

I love Thanksgiving. Growing up, I looked forward to the quiet holiday tucked between my birthday and Christmas, because I could eat all I wanted—an unusual occurrence when competing on a daily basis with six siblings, hungry and mean. But I discovered Thanksgiving was more than abundant food when I celebrated it with a college friend and her family.

I remember sitting with careful posture at a crowded table, wondering what I would talk about with these people who didn't ask a blessing on the food and argued about politics while passing the gravy. I felt like a water balloon, full of bottled-up tears, about to burst.

I thought perhaps hunger motivated my misery: I hadn't taken second helpings because no one else did. Evidently, at this table, it would be inappropriate to eat until stuporous. Or maybe my unhappiness flowed from the absence of pumpkin pie. When the hostess produced chocolate mousse for desert, I barely managed to stifle a gasp of disbelief: No pumpkin pie? What sort of family is this?

Then, unannounced, Aunt Mary danced into my mind. I adored her. She had crooked teeth like mine and listened to me. I smelled her lilac scent and saw her flushed cheeks as she kicked off her shoes after Thanksgiving dinner and performed a Charleston to music on my cousin's transistor radio. Just a flash of memory, then she was gone. The truth hit me. It wasn't pumpkin pie or the opportunity for gluttony I missed. I was homesick.

Every Thanksgiving my family drove from Lake Shore to Provo in a bulging sedan, balancing foil-covered pans of dinner rolls and newspaper-wrapped casseroles, to gather in a church recreation hall with Mom's folks.

It was a large and raucous group: grandma, aunts, uncles, and too many cousins to count, ranging from college students trying to look intellectual to new babies being passed hand to hand. Grandma, Mom, and my aunts ruled the kitchen, laughing and working in a precise choreography, shooing away interlopers looking for a taste of turkey.

A volleyball game with fluid teams ebbed and flowed at one end of the gym. Toddlers, playing tag, ran through the court, disrupting play, dodging between the legs of the players. No one seemed to mind

Uncle Norley's laugh boomed as he and Dad swapped hunting stories; Mr. Potato Head pieces crunched underfoot; and marbles from the Chinese checkers game bounced off the board. In a corner, teenagers clustered to pose and share insider information, banning younger siblings from their circle.

When Aunt Alice didn't finish lining the tables with butcher paper and later wondered why anyone would put walnuts in fruit salad, we noticed. But we reserved judgment; she was from Oregon, after all, and new to the clan.

During the meal, familiar stories were repeated; cousins compared ballooning bellies; and the cooks were applauded. Everyone agreed it was the best meal yet, and Grandpa would have loved it. Grandma prepared packets of food for each family to take home and hugged us to her as we left.

Being thankful is best done when surrounded by loved ones. Over the years, my definition of family has expanded. Dear friends have brightened my favorite holiday; new families have enriched it.

Still, at some point during the happiness of my Thanksgivings, a moment arrives when my mind rushes back to a family-filled gym. Once again I see the smile of my still-young mom and enjoy the antics of her kin.

Remembering Recess

Elementary students carrying backpacks and carefree attitudes pass my house on their way to and from school. They call out and laugh, shedding announcements, art projects, and jackets as mindlessly as the surrounding trees drop leaves. Chasing one another, they yell challenges, jump into puddles, make their own rules. In winter, they stump along with one foot on the curb, the other in the gutter, shattering ice. When the sidewalk is slick, they back up to get a running start on their slide. Sometimes they climb the mounds of dirty snow lining the street and attempt to shoe-ski down.

I envy their energy and imagine them running wild in the freedom of recess. Then I remember Barney Cornaby, my third-grade friend, and the eagerly awaited words of our teacher: "Boys and girls, it's time to get ready for recess. Clear your desks and put your heads down while I choose the line leader. Remember, quiet and cleanliness count."

I jammed my reading book into my desk, plopped my head onto its scratched surface, and curled my disreputable nails into my palms. Listening to stout Mrs. Beale strut up and down the aisles to inspect us, I silently chanted: "Choose me, choose me, choose me." Being selected to lead the class out of the room and down the hall meant a few seconds head start on recess.

The words, "Shirley, you may go to the door," told me Mrs. Beal had once again chosen Miss Perfect as line leader. The rest of us would have to wait until our rows were called. Mine would be last because Gregory Dixon never remembered to wash his ears.

I lived for the moment I emerged into recess from the heavy wooden doors of Lake Shore Elementary School and raced across its playground. First, I sprinted around swings, slides, and teeter-totters, looking like weary soldiers braced for the oncoming attack. Next, I flew by the overflowing drinking fountain Joe Nielson had dammed with gravel and dirt—a habit he couldn't overcome no matter how much time he spent in the principal's office. I ran through the shade of a discouraged sycamore tree and skidded to a stop on the asphalt basketball court. There, I would join hands with Barney to dance with wild abandon for the fifteen precious minutes of recess.

I, big for a 3rd grader, and Barney, small, danced together in perfect syncopation to tunes we sang loudly and off-key. My long legs leaping about in diverse directions, I twirled in delight as he bobbed around me like a drunken grasshopper. Then with hem undone, scabs on each knee, and unruly hair flying in tangles, I boogied around the always spiffy Barney with his pants belted high, shirt buttoned to the top, and hair carefully slicked to the side.

Young and happy, we gave no thought to our appearance, risk of ridicule, or lack of talent. Our lives had not yet been invaded by peer pressure. So we sang and tap-danced with more vigor than rhythm in freewheeling fun we hadn't learned to censor. I have never felt as graceful and invincible as when Barney and I twirled on our toes, floated our arms aloft, and bounded across the court in gravity-defying leaps.

We relished our fifteen minutes of happy-go-lucky hoofing until the custodian rang the tower bell. As we left the noise of the playground and walked through the cool dimness of the hall, past the lunchroom smelling of homemade rolls, and into the rigid rows of the classroom, our songs and pirouettes still sang and bounced inside of us.

A Little Bit of Paradise

Before the Craig Daily Press discontinued the column, *Moffat County Neighbor,* I looked forward to the question, "What's your favorite place in Moffat County?" I enjoyed learning what other people like about where we live. I thought if I were interviewed for the feature, I might dither about three people I'd invite to dinner or the type of music I prefer, but could name my favorite place without hesitation.

Whenever I drive home along Highway 13 or 40, I anticipate my first glimpse of Cedar Mountain. Around town, I lift my eyes to find it. I like the way its profile varies depending on my vantage point. From some locations, it seems to shoot fiercely from the earth, towering high; at others, it appears gentle and approachable; always, it is unique in its isolation.

Joel and I like to walk the well-kept trail that traces the mountain. The path offers a perfect short hike: steep climbs interspersed with long cruising stretches downhill or parallel to the mountain's crest. On the uphill, our hearts pump hard; and our breathing startles the good people in Maybell. The flatter sections permit rhythmic breathing and long, loose steps. Descending, I keep my knees flexed and my toes slightly curled—my new boots are a bit too short, though when I tromped around the store in them, they felt fine. As we hike, we examine the surrounding terrain, noting subtle changes that mark the progress of the seasons.

In the spring, as soon as the trail dries enough to prevent mud from collecting beneath our boots, we go to the mountain. Fresh green unfurls in all directions, softening the world, lifting our winter-weary hearts, cushioning strong-willed wildflowers. We walk to the edge of a steep bluff and peer over at an old eagle nest, hoping to find it occupied this year, but are disappointed.

As summer gains dominance, we leave earlier for our hike, wear cooler clothes, wish we had remembered our sunglasses. Birds powdered with blue group on favored bushes, fretting about our passing. Grasshoppers bounce off our legs. The fields stretching below wear a purposeful green. The sky melts away.

The Cedar Mountain of autumn is transcendent. Understated shades of brown and gold fade into one another. Deer freeze in wide-eyed poses or flee in swift, silent bounds. Indian paintbrush stands crimson and stalwart. We lift our faces, storing up a winter's supply of sun.

Eventually, ice and snow end our weekly walk. We shove hiking boots to the back of the closet, vow to buy snowshoes, and watch from the valley as snow accumulates on our mountain. We imagine it misses us.

We like the people we meet on Cedar Mountain and most of their dogs. We look forward to the lady with the two Labradors: one, old and dignified, approaches slowly and nods his head in greeting; another, young and muscled, with more energy than common sense, bounces up and wriggles with delight, as though meeting us is better than puppy chow.

We step aside for mountain bikers and runners, respecting the effort and skill they are expending. Once we came across an early morning photographer practicing her art. On occasion, we see folks unloading horses from trailers and gearing up for a ride, but we've never met them on the trail. We wouldn't mind.

During bow season this year, we met two hunters and asked where they would be hunting, so we wouldn't interfere. They told us they hadn't seen any bucks and were giving up for the day. They thanked us for our concern and remarked, "We all need to share such a beautiful spot and take care of each other and it. This mountain is something remarkable, isn't it?"

Indeed, it is.

Part 4 Winter

Winter attacks like a skilled basketball team: stuttering and faking to advance, sinking slick shots, defending with sudden blizzards, and rejecting autumn's last-minute attempt to force overtime.

Soon we are listening to Craig's winter symphony: the deep rumble of snowplows and rhythmic scrape of shovels and roof rakes, the moaning tenor of snow blowers, the celery-crunch percussion of frozen snow beneath cautious feet, the deep, silent pause of midnight under a blanket of snow.

We wear boots, hoods, gloves, scarves, and red noses. We propel our bodies on skis, skates, snowshoes, and snow machines. Seeking relief, we travel to California, Nevada, Arizona and marvel at the sight of clean cars traveling on swept pavement.

My entire life, I looked forward to the dramatic, weather-driven splendor of this demanding season. Now, at seventy, I understand that winter, the final stage in nature's cycle, mirrors my life; and, as I enter it, I continue to anticipate the rugged beauty found among its challenges.

Wow, It's Cold

Last Sunday, I raised the blinds as a hardy neighbor walked his dog by our house: an ordinary sight, except for the lowered earflaps on the man's hat and the hound's embarrassment at wearing a red-and-yellow doggy sweater. Fingernail-resistant frost edged our windows, and when Joel opened the door to retrieve the paper, a frigid wind invaded, bullied our heated air, and touched my face with frozen fingers. "Hmm," I thought, "must be a cold one."

Monday morning, I poured a cup of coffee and checked my e-mail. A brother wrote that he'd heard about our low temperatures on the weather channel. "Are you folks in Craig OK?" he asked. I looked out my window at the 8:00 a.m. street scene: children walking to school with red ears and no hats; cars on slick snow trailing geysers of exhaust; a bundled-up fellow riding a bicycle with one hand stuffed in his pocket; a neighbor with a red hat and happy smile, shoveling her sidewalk; two coffee-drinking men in a pickup pulling a trailer loaded with snow machines; a city truck spewing sand at intersections.

Yup. We're all right. When our winters turn bitterly cold and our world feels brittle—as though it would shatter into frozen fragments at a shout—we go on with our lives. But we talk. During a brief stop at the grocery store, I overheard fellow shoppers say: "My dog loves this weather, because we let him sleep inside;" "Even my high school son put on a coat this morning;" and, "Damn truck wouldn't start. Again."

I like thinking I'm tough enough to survive in a place where temperatures can hover well below zero; twenty above feels mild; and thirty degrees with sunshine causes us to exclaim happily and hold our faces to the sun. I learned about the gumption of Moffat County's populace during a meeting at the school district administration office the first winter I worked there. I asked how many snow days were typically called during a school year. Everybody laughed—at length. I thought I noted a tinge of hysteria, but I'm not sure.

Last year, during a cold spell, a neighbor said: "I don't mind the freezing temperatures, but when I walk to work, the constant squeaking gets to me." During a telephone conversation, I shared this amusing comment with a friend who lives in sunny St. George, Utah. A puzzled silence followed.

Since retiring, my appreciation for winter has grown: white, frozen waves camouflaging the earth's nakedness; raucous crows scolding from tree tops; frosting fluffing up on branches, electric lines, and fences. I like wearing a stocking cap over uncombed hair and gliding on cross-country skis through fields of diamonds shadowed by tree branches fuzzy with frost, like antlers in velvet. I'm happy as I pull on snowshoes to hike a silent, white-cloaked Cedar Mountain. And I enjoy one of retired life's greatest pleasures: getting up on a cold-choked morning with no need to rush out into the ice-bound world.

After my sophomore year of college, my parents moved to Lander, Wyoming. During my time at Utah State University and for many years after I married, I traveled to Lander for Christmas. Each time, I draped myself in knitted throws, sat by Dad's wood-burning stove, piled extra quilts on my bed, and complained: "Why," I asked my parents, "would anyone choose to live in this kind of cold?"

Years later, when I told Dad I was moving to Craig, he reminded me of my comments and wondered if I was about to leap "out of the igloo and onto the ice floe."

Yes, I was.

Family Economics, 2008

My husband and I recently joined the fixed-income set. With impeccable timing, we retired as the economy shattered. We'll be fine. We came from large families with blue-collar budgets and parents who insisted we wear it out, save for a rainy day, turn out the lights. I would be more confident about our country weathering the current economic situation if everyone had learned these frugalities when young. But not everybody was raised by graduates of the Great Depression, as Joel and I were.

When I was twelve, the sound of my parents' voices pushed through the kitchen floor to the top bunk of the bedroom below, where I rolled over and stretched. I liked waking to their drifting conversations, but felt uneasy when their voices were loud enough that I could distinguish words, because that meant they were discussing money. Though they agreed on the governing fiscal policy for our household—buy only what you can afford, stay out of debt, save as much as possible—they sometimes disagreed on its application.

In a good month when Dad had worked long, hot hours of overtime at the steel plant, Mom might suggest they spend the extra earnings on something frivolous, perhaps a vacuum that sucked more than it spewed. Dad would argue for making a double house payment. Usually the debate ended with Dad's oft-repeated sentiment, "I'm just trying to keep a roof over our heads. We'll be lucky if we don't all end up in the poorhouse."

When young, I imagined the poorhouse as our neighbor's decrepit barn, full of people dressed in grain sacks with signs reading "the poor" hung around their necks. They huddled in empty stalls, wailed, and chewed on turnips. This image guaranteed my cooperation during the family meetings held when Dad was on strike or laid off.

First, Mom would explain there had been another lay-off, and while Dad looked for work, we would need to cut back on spending. Her seven children, knowing the routine, would look solemn, but feel no anxiety. She next announced the non-debatable reductions: We would stop the newspaper and quit going to the Dairy Queen. There would be only one birthday present, and despite recent promises, we would continue to be one of the few families in our rural area without a TV. I hid my joy when told that I would have to stop piano lessons, but felt sad that we could no longer go swimming at Arrowhead, a local indoor pool where I loved watching the sleekness with which my dad swam.

After we heard the mandatory cuts, we were asked for other suggestions, but usually could think of none, though I remember one of us once suggesting that perhaps we could save money if we bathed less often.

Now, during the holiday season of 2009, I fret about the unemployed and uninsured, about foreclosures and mounting credit-card debt. I think about my loved ones. I would like to share my parents' wisdom with them, without seeming to deliver a lecture. I wish they would discover, as I did when young, that economizing doesn't mean the absence of fun and that paring a budget can be a beneficial lesson when children are allowed to participate.

I hope that across our country, in response to our economic upheaval, family meetings are being held.

The Fine Art of Giving

Once again Christmas commercials feature perfect gifts joyfully given and joyfully received. Never in my life have I given a gift that caused jubilation. No matter how much thought, money, and time I spend selecting a present, I doubt myself: What was I thinking? Did I buy the needlepoint kit for my outdoorsy friend because she would like it, because I wanted it, or because shopping made my feet ache?

I'm particularly inept at choosing gifts for group exchanges or Secret Santa festivities. I remember purchasing a book of Life Savers for a gift exchange at a friend's Christmas party in sixth grade. With Santa on the cover, it looked festive, and—what the heck—everybody likes Life Savers. As the party approached, I began to worry. One friend was taking Cheery Cherry lipstick; another chose a ponytail barrette shaped like a butterfly. What was I thinking with my babyish gift? After much fussing, I stayed home and crunched Life Savers until my teeth ached.

I'm also plagued by gift exchange rules: a recommended price or the specification of a white elephant. When I comply, others don't; when I don't, others do. Either way, as my gift is opened, I stick my head in a houseplant. I once attended an all female Christmas party where joke gifts were to be exchanged. The guests exclaimed happily as they opened their gifts: decorative candles, See's chocolates, holly-bedecked hand towels.

An appalled silence greeted my contribution: a jar of water holding a dead gold fish.

Even when I manage to choose an appropriate gift, I err in other ways. In fifth grade, I drew Kirk Moore's name for the class Christmas party. I hated Kirk: In October, he had challenged me to a bicycle race. I was about to win when he ran into my back tire on purpose, I wrecked, and my knee was scarred. Now I had to give him a gift?

Mumbling and mean-spirited, I bought a bag of marbles and wrapped it in recycled paper my thrifty mom had carefully folded and saved the previous Christmas. Instead of thanks, I received hoots of laughter when the despicable thug discovered last year's to-and-from designation written on the recycled wrap and showed it to one and all. Later, in the lunch line, I pinched him, hard; and when questioned, lied about it.

I'm equally flummoxed by birthday gifts, retirement gifts, wedding gifts, and events specifying "Please, no gifts"—a request ignored by everybody but me.

During my teenage years, my best friend was the most gifted person I knew. She received presents from Santa Claus, St. Valentine, the Easter Bunny, the Good Witch, and Father Pilgrim. She continued the tradition for her children and grandchildren, wrapping a multitude of gifts each year. I experience respiratory problems just thinking about her never-ending task, and she's developed a nervous tic.

I atone for my gift-selection errors by occasionally bestowing gifts for no reason other than fondness for the recipient. I feel happier and more confident selecting non-required gifts: genuine surprise usually trumps, "Good grief, why did she think I'd like this?"

A rough-and-tumble child gave me the best lesson I've ever received about giving, if I would just remember it.

The day before Christmas vacation, I stood on an icy playground, braced against a snow-flecked wind, keeping an eye on children who happy-danced with excitement. Feeling a tug on my sleeve, I looked down at the beaming face of Freddy, a young boy of exuberance, who sometimes visited with me in my office about the need for rules. He peeled off a mitten and opened his hand to reveal a soggy piece of fudge, melting in his sweaty palm. "Here, Principal, my mom made this, and I saved one of my pieces for you, because I like you."

A humble offering from an open heart: the perfect gift, given and received with joy.

Montgomery Wards Catalogue

Because we lived without television and far from town, my siblings and I didn't have store displays or TV commercials to help us decide what we wanted for Christmas. Instead, the inspiration for our letters to Santa Claus came from the Montgomery Wards Christmas catalogue. The catalogue arrived in mid-November to hosannas of joy and died a quiet, rumpled death by Christmas Eve. In between, it dominated our holiday season.

Soon after Halloween, fights broke out over a chore we usually scrambled to avoid: trudging a quarter mile to get the mail. We each wanted to be the first to touch the Christmas catalogue's slick pages, breathe its acrid smell, and read its tantalizing descriptions of toys, candy, and clothing.

For five weeks, the increasingly bedraggled catalogue circulated from hand to hand. Mom reminded us daily, with diminishing holiday spirit, that we couldn't study it during meals. We condemned the unknown ne'er-do-well who dropped it in the bathtub, rendering several pages unreadable. At night, when we should have been sleeping, we whispered excited comments to one another about the treasures it contained.

Having seven children and little discretionary money, Mom told us Santa had a ten-dollar limit per child. We each made lengthy lists, agonizing over whether to eliminate Mr. Potato Head or Lincoln Logs. We sought one another's advice and argued the merits of our selections. Finally, our decisions made, we wrote our letters to Santa and hoped.

When we earned spending money by picking fruit or hoeing sugar beets, we bought gifts for each other from the catalogue as well. After a few weeks, mysterious markings known only by their creators appeared on its sticky pages. One year, Bob tormented Carolyn and me by putting our initials next to several items in the catalogue, leading us to think (A) those were the things he might buy for us and (B) he wasn't very bright. A week later, we noticed he had circled in red crayon a half-pound box of cherry chocolates for me and a necklace of plastic beads for Carolyn. Perfect choices.

On Christmas morning, Bob snickered and gloated when we ripped open our presents from him and discovered he hadn't chosen anything he'd marked. Instead, Carolyn received a sampler set of twenty-five tiny tubes of perfume, and I got a winter hat I could stick my ponytail through—completely inedible.

When I was twelve, we moved ten miles away to Spanish Fork with its multiple shopping opportunities: Forsey's Five and Dime, J.C. Penney, and Woolworths. The Montgomery Ward Christmas catalogue lost its importance; the ten-dollar limit drifted away. It seemed to me that with their disappearance, much of the anticipation of the Christmas season vanished as well. I found I missed the colorful catalogue, the snowballing excitement that arrived with it, and the whispered conversations that flowed between our beds.

Always Winter

I first experienced the deceit of Rabbit Ears, a mountain pass near my new home, when Joel and I drove from Denver to Craig on a balmy June day. Air flowed warm under an immense sky, and new green growth waved us on—until Rabbit Ears. As we began to ascend the pass, fat flakes fell so heavily and persistently through sunshine that I had to stretch out of my window to knock clumps of snow off the struggling wipers. Later, when I described the trip to a long-time Craig resident, he responded, "It's always bad on Rabbit Ears."

Fourteen years later, I've accepted his truth and experienced it many times: slow speeds and tense shoulders, white-knuckles and mild profanity, freewheeling spins and whose-idea-was-this.

On one snow-bound trip, frozen roads glistened ice-slick in the sun as I maintained a safe distance from the car in front of me. The driver behind also kept a sensible distance and showed no interest in passing. Our caravan traveled across the mountain without difficulty. As we neared the descent to Muddy Gap, an SUV came up from behind and leapfrogged us, one by one. The driver—holding the steering wheel, a hot dog and a giant slurpee—saluted dismissively. We passed him later: he was standing on the side of the road, gesturing at his vehicle buried in a bank of snow, talking to a patrolman, and mopping away slurpee. I censored my salute.

I have a love-hate relationship with snowplows. On occasion, I've followed their lights slowly, but safely, across the mountain and felt gratitude. But I'm panic-stricken when a plow barrels around a curve toward me at night: lights flashing, snow flying, blade crowding my lane. The mammoth machines cause the butterflies in my stomach to stop fluttering and begin clogging.

Sometimes, when winter conditions are normal on Rabbit Ears—berserk winds, inscrutable snow, cars playing pinball—Joel and I pass parking areas thronged with happy people unloading snow machines, snowshoes, or skis. What are they thinking? They've driven in these conditions to play in the snow?

Must be from Craig.

Last year in mid-October, we drove home through Missouri and Kansas in our rear-wheel-drive car without snow tires or chains. A bright sun in a clear sky guided us most of the way. Then, five miles before Rabbit Ears, a blizzard exploded and carpeted the road with ice. Joel slowed, concentrated, and kept us moving up the first incline. We thought we might miss Christmas, but didn't doubt we'd make it home.

As a pickup pulled into the other lane to pass us, it's rear-end began sashaying like the backside of a puppy. It cleared us, then spun out, forcing Joel to tap the brakes. We slewed off the road onto the shoulder. The truck corrected and continued shaking its booty around the curve. We sat stalled, momentum lost.

Joel, capable of vocalizing angrily over minor irritants, becomes calm and efficient when faced with a problem. I become tense and speak in squeaks. "Janet, get over here. You'll have to drive while I push the car back on the road and we get going. It's in gear, but it won't go anywhere until I push. Just steer and take it easy on the gas once we're straightened out." Squeaking my agreement, and thinking the matter urgent, I climbed from my seat to the driver's side, rather than going around, a feat hampered by my long legs and terror.

Once in place, I clutched the wheel while Joel slid the back-end onto the iced road. I straightened the wheel and tenderly pressed on the gas. Nothing happened. Joel pushed. I gave it a little more gas. We didn't move. "Did you take it out of gear?" Joel thundered. No, I didn't. Not deliberately. But I must have bumped it out during my plucky seat crossing.

Gear engaged, we tried again; Joel pushed; the car inched forward. Through the open window, I heard huffing and puffing, then calm instructions: "OK, a little more gas."

The car began to move at a steady pace. I gave it more gas. Wow! We were going to make it!

A desperate roar ended my self-congratulations: "Janet, what the bleep are you doing? I can't bleeping run up the bleeping mountain! Stop! S-T-O-P!!" I looked in the rear-view mirror at a tiny, open-mouthed figure, waving its arms and fading from sight.

It's always bad on Rabbit Ears.

A Christmas Pageant

I loved the small, rural community that sheltered me and the elementary school that anchored it. During the fifties, I attended school in a red brick building with creaky wooden floors, hissing radiators, and banks of windows darkened by roller shades. George Washington and Abraham Lincoln kept solemn watch over the classrooms where we sat in wooden desks attached to rails.

After Thanksgiving vacation, a Christmas tree stood tall in the cafeteria, radiating its outdoor smell of pine, adorned with ornaments created from construction paper and good-tasting paste. Spilled glitter sparkled on oiled floors, and children's voices practicing holiday music drifted through the halls.

This was a magical time when the farm children of Lake Shore Elementary began to prepare for the annual Christmas Pageant, a gala attended by parents and grandparents, aunts and uncles, brothers and sisters, former teachers, church elders, senior citizens, and, on one occasion, a dog that wandered in through an open door. All students at the school participated, graduating from minor to starring roles as they progressed from kindergarten to sixth grade. I made this journey with the same twenty-one classmates: nine girls and twelve boys, my extended family.

The task of kindergarten and first-grade students was to be lovable, a fail-proof plan. They wandered around the stage in angel, deer, or elf costumes, waving at their parents, tying their shoes, pushing their self-crafted hats out of their eyes, and forgetting the lyrics they'd rehearsed for weeks. Those in second and third grade performed group dances. They tripped on their tin soldier or snowflake getups, shoved slower hoofers out of their way, and sometimes, overcome by vigorous twirling, fell off the stage.

Students in fourth and fifth grade graduated to partner dancing. I remember warbling a song about winter winds blowing and night skies snowing while performing a skating routine. We wore earmuffs created by room mothers from yarn, paper cups and cotton batting, making us look more like invading space aliens than winter revelers. As we went through our paces, my face glowed red from the exertion of lugging my partner Glen Gunderson around the floor. Glenn smelled like manure and talked in a gurgle that made me compulsively clear my throat. Teachers always paired us as dancing partners because he was the only boy close to my height. A hefty boy, he was a heavy load to pull through the steps of a dance while singing and hissing, "Step-glide, Glenn, step-glide, GLIDE, Glen, GLIDE."

The solos and speaking parts were assigned to the sixth grade and eagerly sought, especially the role of Mary in the nativity tableaux, a staging that ended the show as the audience stood and sang "Silent Night." I promised myself I'd stop swearing, pinching and spitting, if I was asked to be Mary. It worked. When Mr. Wadsen announced the roles to his sixth-grade class, I was a dancing holly sprig, one of nine singing angels—the only one with a speaking part—Mrs. Claus in the Santa's workshop scene, and the Blessed Mother Mary.

The night of the performance, the holly plants were to cavort in green stocking feet. I missed the word green, so wore red socks to highlight the glossy berries dotting my green tutu. Surely the audience wouldn't notice the ragged hole in one heel. Mrs. Huff, the director, suffering from nerves, became hysterical at the sight of my feet and told me to take off my disgraceful socks and dance barefoot.

Next, the nine singing angels warbled *The First Noel* after which

I bellowed out my much-practiced speaking part, "Hosanna, hosanna, hosanna on high." In the excitement of the moment, I became confused and shouted out a friend's name instead, so my line came out, "Johanna, Johanna, Johanna on high." Mrs. Huff's eyes rolled back in her head.

Mrs. Claus went off without a hitch, except for the excitement caused by Pete Madsen as Mr. Claus. Pete stepped on a kindergarten elf, whose blubbering drowned out my lines.

At last, the grand finale, the nativity scene: I donned a dark blue, velvet gown my mother had fashioned from a formal she found at a thrift store and draped a soft white shawl over my hair. While the cast sang "Away in a Manger," I took a baby doll wrapped in a hand-crocheted covering and felt my way across the darkened stage to my seat on a bale of hay. I smelled my skating partner, Glenn of the barnyard, when he took his place next to me as Joseph, and sensed the assembling wise men and shepherds, classmates all, and solemnly subdued.

The song faded; Glenn gurgled and placed his hand on my shoulder; the shepherd's knelt with bowed heads. I sat up straight and cuddled the doll in my arms, bouncing it slightly just as I did when Mom let me hold my baby brother. The pianist sounded the first chords of "Silent Night." The audience stood and began to sing, and the spotlight hit us.

As I looked up, proud to show this special baby to all these people I knew and liked, I caught a loving smile on my mother's face. Something flared inside me, and for the first time, I experienced the real spirit of Christmas. I was flooded with good will, a feeling of peace, a sense of belonging. I glanced down at my baby. "Merry Christmas," I whispered, "Merry Christmas."

I Refuse to Resolve

I look forward to the fresh feel of January when stark coldness freezes bad stuff—germs, jaywalking, poor posture—and encourages new beginnings. I contemplate ways to better myself: I could pursue intellectual, activities seek consistency with my grooming, sew without profanity.

I like such thoughts; they make me feel virtuous. But I haven't formalized a New Year's resolution since 1955. I was eleven that year, and I vowed to quit eating candy for twelve months. When family and friends questioned my sanity, I quoted a line I'd heard in church about the strength I'd gain through sacrifice.

I knew folks would be appalled if I told the truth. I was going to give up eating candy so I could save it until the next Christmas, when I would have more candy than any child in the world. No self-sacrificing saint, I was planning an orgy. I pursued my objective with vigor and immediacy. I cleaned out the bottom drawer of my dresser, lined it with waxed paper, and made my first donation—a partially eaten candy cane I had been enjoying when struck by the wisdom of amassing bonbons for a binge.

For twelve months, I saved every sweet that came my way. Boxes of small pastel hearts reading "4-U" and "Be Mine" nestled next to puffy marshmallow bunnies and chocolate eggs. Pieces of licorice distributed by Mr. Ralphs on the last day of school stuck to cotton candy from the Fourth of July. Kraft caramels, candy corn, and miniature Snickers bars marked Halloween. I threw in the gumdrops that formed the tail feathers of the apple turkey I made for Thanksgiving with the anchoring toothpicks still attached.

I bought candy as always, but rather than chowing down, I added the purchases to my burgeoning stash. I reserved one corner of the drawer for the treats Mom made: divinity, fudge, taffy, peanut brittle. The fudge hardened to jawbreaker status and the divinity developed green spots, but I thought they'd still be edible. In my frenzy to fill the drawer as Christmas neared, I began to save cookies as well. Once, as I headed for my room with a layer of caramel frosting from my piece of Dad's birthday cake, Mom stopped me with three grimly-spoken words: "Don't you dare."

Each night, while other children enjoyed bedtime stories or kneeled to say their prayers, I opened my drawer, inhaled the mixed odors of chocolate, peppermint, and cinnamon, then counted. I made my younger sister Barbara watch as I added the day's take to the running total I marked on the side of the drawer. She knew if ever my count didn't match that tally, her life was on the line. In the final months, the count took longer, so we got little sleep and began to do poorly in school.

Christmas Eve, after the party at Grandma's, I dumped the drawer on my bed and began to chew. Christmas day, after Santa and a holiday breakfast, the binge continued. One day later, I began to share with Barbara. Two days later, I looked away when she sneaked more. Three days later, as I sprawled on my bed among mounds of crumbs and candy wrappers, Barbara told me I looked like Anderson's cow that time it got the bloat. Chocolate smears smudged my yellow complexion, my tongue swelled until it protruded, sugar crusted my lips. I gasped and burped and moaned. I gave up.

"Be careful what you wish for," we caution one another. Amen and amen. I never made another New Year's resolution. I was afraid I would keep it.

On February Fourteenth

I achieved enlightenment while waiting for a friend to join me in a restaurant as I eavesdropped on a conversation between two ladies, whose voices drifted from the next booth.

One woman complained that her husband was driving her crazy: he gave her practical gifts, ate sauerkraut with his steak, and threw his dirty socks under the bed. Her friend advised her to forgive her spouse's quirks. After all, he wasn't raised in her family with its habitual behaviors, traditions, and preferences. If he liked his chicken charred, that's probably how his mother cooked it; and she should cut him some slack.

What an eye-opener. Could Joel's upbringing be the reason he enjoys driving with the gas gauge on empty, saves little pieces of soap to someday merge into big pieces of soap, and turns up the heat so he can walk around barefoot in his workout shorts in January?

Maybe. But I'm not convinced his peculiarities flow from his family. After all, he was raised in a computer-free home; so where does he get the idea I should enjoy watching him surf the Internet? Forensics weren't important on the TV shows he grew up with: the Lone Ranger and the Little Rascals didn't bother much with DNA and carpet fibers. So why does he continue to concentrate on the TV—where an expert is about to solve a kidnapping based on mosquito larvae in the grille of a Plymouth—when I announce that a little girl just wandered into our yard and drank from our birdbath

He grew up with sisters who surely asked his opinion of their hairstyles. Why didn't he develop response skills? When he's in a hurry, and I say I should do something with my disheveled hair before leaving, he tells me not to worry: my hair looks great. Another day, with time to spare, he says my hair looks flat, except for the bird nest in the back.

But such foibles are few and inconsequential when I think about the good qualities he has: I value his work ethic, appreciate his way with children, respect his professionalism, admire his friendliness, and enjoy his sense of humor. He introduced me to community involvement, informed my worldview, and taught me most of what I know about technology. He likes me and forgives my faults—except for my inability to read a map and road signs simultaneously.

Many years ago, a divorce behind me, I drove pine-scented roads to a ski resort in the Sierra Nevada Mountains to attend a workshop on effective teaching techniques. Throughout the course, the instructor demonstrated strategies for randomly grouping students for discussion or project work, as an occasional change from teacher-assigned grouping. To do this, she had us form groups based on different criteria: find others of approximately your height, those having the same pet as you, or those wearing a similar shoe style. No matter what common attribute she specified, I noticed an outgoing, big-shouldered guy with an easy laugh in all my groups.

I worried about his hearing and thought he must have eye problems. When grouping by hair of a similar length, he was at my elbow; when finding those with the same hobby, he followed me into a knitting group. Others came and went, but he seemed to think the two of us were perfectly matched on any given qualifier.

Joel and I have been in one another's group since that first meeting; and we still match on the criteria that matter. I was the one with faulty hearing and weak eyes.

A Valentine for Siblings

"Be kind to your brothers and sisters, " a high school teacher once advised, "Their life span parallels yours. If you're good to them, they'll be part of your life for more years than your parents, spouse, or children."

When I was younger—engaged in teasing, tattling, and wrestling with my six siblings—I would have scorned such an idea. Who'd want to be stuck with that throng of thugs forever? But when something threatened one of them, I was devastated. I remember worrying myself sick about Carolyn.

My older sister was an athletic eleven when rheumatic fever forced her to spend five months in bed in the late 1940's. She couldn't get up, even for the bathroom. Bob and I were intrigued: meals in bed served on a tray, big sulfa tablets mashed in honey, the bedpan. For Carolyn, it was prison.

One warm afternoon, Mom suggested that Carolyn, who was serving the second month of her sentence, might like me to read to her. I carried a book into her large, light-filled bedroom made as pleasant as possible on a limited budget. Glass wind chimes hung outside a screen door that provided a cool breeze and a view of the side lawn. An assortment of perfume bottles filled with colored water decorated the windowsills, creating rainbows that shimmered around the room. From a cage suspended in the corner, two canaries fussed in a neighborly way.

The paper dolls we had played with earlier sprawled in various stages of undress atop the bedspread.

Carolyn agreed I could practice my reading on her, but none of that baby stuff. Deep into *The Five Little Peppers and How They Grew*, a selection that elicited only a minor eyeball roll from my weak sister, I didn't notice that the family cat had sneaked in with me. It stealthily circled the room before leaping onto the birdcage, claws scrabbling toward its alarmed, wing-beating prey. While I sat open-mouthed, Carolyn ignored Dr. Moody's repeated warnings about the danger to her heart of sudden movement and sprang into action.

"Damn it," she shrieked, a daughter loyal to our profane father, and leaped out of bed, swinging her pillow. Cat vanquished, door slammed; birds screeching but safe; she flounced back to bed, fixed me with a threatening look, and described in detail what would happen to me if I told, anyone, ever, that she got out of bed.

I had bigger worries: I thought my lack of attention would cause her death. When she fell asleep, exhausted, I left the room, but kept creeping back to check her breathing every five minutes all afternoon, my heart frozen from my fear of losing her.

Recently, I showed a friend a photograph taken of my siblings and me the previous summer at a reunion. As I named each, I imagined how she saw us: faces lined with wrinkles, some slightly stooped, some overweight, some bald, nothing remarkable about any of us. But that's not what I see. When I study the photograph, the years fade away, and I see us as we were: energy-filled, happy, and friends even as we squabbled. I see brothers and sisters who know me completely—the good, the bad, and the ugly—and still love me. I give thanks that over the years we've been nice to each other, that they've been part of my life as long as I remember.

Sometimes in dreams I return to the homes and years I shared with my brothers and sisters. We're usually gathered in the kitchen: I sense the presence of our parents; I hear laughter; and I relax into the sense of belonging I feel when with my family.

Queen of the Trampoline

In the 1950's, before the advent of Title Nine and competitive athletic programs for women, most girls in the physical education classes at Spanish Fork Junior High School avoided intense play and sweating.

Somehow, the rowdy girls of grade school, who competed fiercely and boasted loudly, transformed into a giggling gaggle more interested in watching the boys horse around at the other end of the gym than in the exhortations of Miss Erickson, our militant PE teacher. I'd like to say I remained true to myself and participated as fully and aggressively as I had when younger, but I didn't. I joined the pack. Decked out in regulation blue rompers that bagged below my knees, I tittered with my friends, running, batting, or dribbling only when necessary and always with decorum.

Then, during my eighth-grade year on a snow-driven day that forced us inside, I executed a trick that caught the attention of everybody in the gym: boys, girls, teachers, and a custodian who wandered by. The school had purchased a trampoline: an unknown and amazing contraption in our small town. It stood in splendor on the stage as we girls straggled in for roll call and distracted us from the boys goosing each other across the way.

Throughout the period, squads of six girls then six boys were sent to the stage to learn basic moves on the new piece of equipment, while everybody else continued creating mayhem on the gym floor. My best friend Sharlene and I were in the first group. Miss Erickson asked Carol Johnson, a popular girl who defied tradition and excelled at all things athletic, to demonstrate safe jumping and stopping for us. Then she called on me to be the first to duplicate Carol's moves. I climbed aboard and skittered like a crab across the stretched surface, my face flaming red with embarrassment while Sharlene encouraged me, "You can do it, Janet. You can do it. I think."

I began to bounce. Surprised by the elasticity of the trampoline's response, I gasped, bent my knees, pushed off with more vigor, flailed my arms, and gained altitude. "Whee!" flew unbidden from my mouth. I pushed harder, flew higher, and watched the amazed faces around the trampoline grow larger as I lit and smaller as I rose to new heights. Unbelievable: I was having fun in PE.

Motion on the floor froze; the sound of bouncing balls ceased; every eye watched me as I soared. Grinning like a crazed Jack-o-lantern, ponytail lifting aloft on my descents, I finally heard Miss Erickson's repeated command: "You've jumped enough, Janet. Execute a stop and get off."

One more bounce: I bounded with all my strength, whooped as I took flight, then came down for a stop. I hit straight-legged and off-balance, torpedoed forward—head down bottom up—and sproinged to a stop, my skull wedged between two of the springs that connected the mat to the frame.

Miss Erickson blasted her whistle; Mr. Beck came running from the gym floor; the custodian sprinted toward the office. Sharlene crouched next to my immobile head: "Janet, talk to me. Are you OK? Are you dead?" I braced my arms and tried to wriggle my head. I was fine: I could breathe. My neck worked, and my head had moved. I knew I could yank it out, but didn't. I felt safe upside down: like an ostrich with its head buried in sand, as long as I was stuck, I could pretend no one could see my rear end waving in the breeze.

I don't remember being shy or hesitant about trying new physical activities in elementary school; I think I developed my hesitancy to do so when I climbed onto that trampoline in eighth grade and shut down a program at Spanish Fork Junior High School until the limits of the school's liabilities could be ascertained.

I earned a new nickname that day; my friends began calling me Bottoms Up.

Beneath Our Feet

On a frozen February morning in my sixty-eighth year, I stepped bare-footed onto the toe-numbing tile floor in our kitchen and instantly thought of the home where I was raised.

In the past, when my siblings and I talked fondly about our childhood home, built by pioneer ancestors on the shores of Utah Lake, our mother would fake a shudder and shake her head. Perhaps she was thinking about the flooring in the old house.

The living room had the only welcoming floor, thanks to Mom's hard work. She could take the humblest cast-offs and with time and skill make something beautiful from them, even the worn-out clothing of her children. From our discards, she cut lengths of fabric that she sewed together and then braided into fat plaits of multi-colored fabric. Next, using a curved needle, she hand-sewed these thick braids into oval rugs where one color faded into another in perfect harmony. The grandest rug of all, sixteen-feet long and nine-feet wide, sat on the painted-board floor of the living room, the only carpet we ever had.

The rest of the floors lacked the appeal of the living room, especially the wooden porch that clung to the front of the house as though afraid of being dropped. It was a haphazard, slanting affair of rough uneven boards pocked by escaping nails where we stubbed our barefoot toes and snagged our winter boots. Bob amused himself my entire third-grade summer by throwing me to its floor and dragging me about, resulting in a condition he cleverly called splinter butt.

The kitchen boasted a level floor but had a nightmarish quality. Between working swing shifts at Ironton Steel and running a small farm, Dad worked as hard as Mom, but without her knack for home decoration. When he decided to tile the kitchen floor, he went at it with his usual uninhibited zeal: singing as he put down linoleum squares and cursing as he ripped them out.

When he was finished, the gray, white, and brown speckled floor was impressive—until we walked on it. With each step the black tar used as bonding material oozed up between the squares, belching and befouling the new surface. For weeks, it glopped here and there and dried in swirling, 3-d patterns: intriguing to children, horrible to Mom. She'd dreamed of a Better-Housekeeping floor, but had to live with the creature from the black lagoon. The most dreaded Saturday chore in the family was scrubbing away at the tar protrusions with scratchy pads of steel wool, a losing battle.

Our bedroom floors were killingly cold in the winter because the heat of the living room and kitchen was never allowed to reach them. To protect our feet from frostbite, my two sisters and I tried to avoid contact with the frigid floor. We'd spring as though on pogo sticks until we could collapse on our beds and argue about who made it in the fewest moves. Carolyn always won, not because she was the best hopper, but because she was the toughest.

The bathroom floor truly tested our pluck. Due to my dad's handicap as a handyman, this room was a continual work in progress. Both plumbing and wiring progressed sporadically and, often, ineffectually. We grew used to the sound of Dad in the bathroom, whistling, thumping, and swearing. When we had to use the room, we maneuvered through scattered tools, abandoned plumbing parts, and the large metal bucket we filled in the tub, which was plumbed, to flush the toilet, which wasn't.

For a few weeks, trips to the bathroom were even more alarming because large portions of the floor had been ripped out so Dad could work on the son-of-a-bitching-bastard sewer line. And if he had been doing electrical work, this obstacle course had to be negotiated in total darkness because someone kept wandering off with the emergency flashlight.

We left Lake Shore long ago, and my parents have been dead for years. But I often think of Mom's answer when I asked, "Didn't you like our Lake Shore house?"

"I did," she replied, "I enjoyed it and the husband and children who lived there with me; but I used to think hell couldn't be any worse than living in that house while your father remodeled it.

The Buzzing of a Fly

Mrs. Cornaby never left her seat; she didn't need to. She commanded her tenth-grade English students with personality and intelligence, not proximity. Much of what I learned in her class informs my life to this day.

At the start of second semester, having convinced us we were not beginning a unit on "pomes" but "po-ems," Mrs. Cornaby made us read one. More alarmingly, she didn't question us about form, meter, or rhyme, but asked what we thought the poet was trying to tell us. The message of the poem in question, "I heard a fly buzz—when I died" by Emily Dickinson, seemed straightforward to me: a lady died and just before doing so, a pesky fly got in the room and bothered her before anyone could swat it. I learned to look beyond the literal in poetry when a quiet boy, new to our class, explained his idea: the poet was talking about the way our memories and minds latch onto unimportant details, even during the most important of events.

Well. Our class finally had a thinker.

I never forgot his interpretation, and throughout my life, I accumulated evidence that supported it.

I often ask former students who contact me, "What do you remember about my class?" Their responses are quick and disconcerting. They seldom comment on my calm classroom, clear explanations, or creative activities. Instead, they remember that I blubbered when I read *Old Yeller* to them; that I once taught an entire period with my slacks unzipped; or that I dropped a cake, home-made and painstakingly decorated by a room mother, on Billy Carson's head.

Raymond, an amiable but uninspired scholar when I taught him in ninth grade, recalled that I began most of my questions with "so" as in "So, Ray, what happened to your homework this time?" A poised young mother, who laughed and played raucously in fourth grade, told me she remembered the way my shoes always matched. I still don't know if she had admired my attempts at color-coordination or the mental alertness that enabled me to wear the same style on each foot.

I accept the answers they give me, because, like theirs, my memory often elevates the unimportant over the meaningful. When I was twelve, our home burned to a blackened heap two days after Christmas. The weeks to come revealed our losses, large and small, but the night of the fire, in a strange bed, I mourned our Christmas tree. I realized that our life with its comforting structures had been torn apart, that Dad's dream of freedom from house payments had died, and that Mom had lost house-beautification projects she had worked on for years. But I cried over a Christmas tree.

Years later, on a cold November day, I made my way through the cafeteria line in the Student Union Building of Utah State University, where I was a junior. Taking a seat at a table cluttered with trays and friends, I thought I heard screams and indistinct shouts. Around the room, heads popped up and necks swiveled as the sounds grew in volume, became alarming. A male student wearing a red windbreaker burst into the cafeteria, waving his arms as though shooing wasps, voice breaking, calling: "They shot him. They shot him."

President Kennedy was dying.

I grew up a bit that day, took a giant step away from the self-absorbed student I had been; but when I remember that afternoon, one of the first things to come back is that the student messenger wore a jacket just like my boyfriend's.

So I enjoy the anecdotes my former students relate—resisting the impulse to probe for more meaningful feedback on my strategies, my content, or my organization—because a skillful high school teacher asked her class to think about the buzzing of a fly.

A Moderate Hearing Loss

A couple of years ago, my husband Joel began mumbling, running his words together willy-nilly; all my grandchildren seemed to need speech therapy; and waiters whispered the night's specials as if revealing classified information. I knew I'd begun to miss words and phrases during conversations, but blamed the mutter-mouths surrounding me. Then I telephoned a niece and realized the deficiency was mine.

Pauline answered the phone cautiously—when elderly relatives call, it's usually to report a loved one's death, illness, or befuddlement. I punched up the volume on my phone—the pesky thing hadn't been working well—and assured Pauline none of the old folks had broken a hip. I then asked for her address so Joel and I could visit when we drove through Wyoming on vacation.

It took three repetitions, the dear girl increasing her volume each time, before I understood her house number. We then embarked on the street name: I concentrated. Pauline yelled. "Hail Mary," I said when I finally understood her, "that's an unusual name for a street."

"No!" she bellowed, "No!! It's Kilmarie: k as in kitten, i as in idiot…" After I hung up, I told my husband I had a hearing problem. He hid his surprise.

Many of my ancestors wrestled with hearing aids and asked, "What? What'd you say?" with varying degrees of irritation. Aunt Vivian continually groped about her ample bust line for the box that powered her aid, needing to "change the damn batteries again." Grandma Hall resorted to a hearing trumpet from a garage sale, preferring it to gadgets that magnified the sound of her chewing until she thought she was dining with King Kong. Though increasingly deaf, Mom wore no aid. Instead, in her practical way, she asked others to "Come closer or talk louder so I can hear you." Dad sported an aid that sometimes fell out of his ear during church and rolled two pews over, squealing like a stuck pig, causing fellow worshippers to convulse with suppressed laughter.

Knowing my heritage, last February, I made an appointment to have my hearing tested. As John, a kind-eyed audiologist, explained the testing he would do, I listened so intently my skull trembled: if I followed his directions exactly, perhaps my hearing would get an A, and I'd live happily every after. I donned headphones, gripped an electronic buzzer, and listened for random tones. To my relief, I heard one, then another, and another. My thumb bounced on the buzzer as rapidly as Louis Armstrong pressed valves on his trumpet—then I grew worried. Was I imagining the sounds? Surely John wouldn't transmit continual tones; perhaps he was tricking me. Craftily, I let my thumb rest, but there—a pitch so soft it might have been a sick gnat. I flew into action again. It was exhausting. Next, John pronounced words at different volumes into my headset and I repeated them: easy words like overcome and red. Or was that overdone and head?

John delivered the verdict gently: enough loss in both ears to warrant hearing aids. He then showed me a small device that sprouted thin wires and explained it could help me return to a nuanced life. The gizmo also carried an impressive price tag that Medicare and most private insurers don't cover. I considered just hanging a sign around my neck: "Moderate hearing loss. Please yell."

I joke about my hearing problem because laughing is more socially acceptable than wailing, but I've learned that any degree of deafness can cause embarrassment, inhibit interactions, and damage one's dignity. So I purchased the hearing aids; and they've made a difference for me.

But what about those for whom the expense is prohibitive? If they can't afford assisted hearing, we might lose them, their personalities, and their contributions. They may fade into isolation and loneliness; and if that happens, we all lose

The Puzzle of Pills

I try to schedule my annual physical during the winter, though sometimes it slips my mind. I think I forget because I know an appointment with my doctor could mean a new prescription, which would cause me to sulk for days as I wallow in my dislike of taking pills.

After my mother's death, my dad disposed of her many prescriptions. He thought the plethora of pills—big, small, yellow, white, capsules and tablets—contributed to her death. Dad never questioned the home remedies recommended by his grandmother—oatmeal baths for chicken pox, licorice paste for corns, onion juice for earaches; and Pepto Bismol, Epsom salts, or witch hazel for all else. But if he had to swallow a pill, his demise was imminent. He once told me that aspirin had crossed his lips, but only to quiet my mother.

I inherited Dad's distrust of pills. I resist when a doctor wants to prescribe a daily tablet into infinity: "Maybe I could lower my cholesterol by making better food choices," I bargain, though past efforts to live without ice cream and eggnog tipped me toward insanity.

When I read the information sheets for new prescriptions, I fall into a tizzy: Side effects may include abdominal pain, nausea, and liver problems. I should seek immediate medical attention if my ankles or tongue swell, my eyes or skin turn yellow, or I stop breathing. "Wow, those are some mean side effects," I think, "I'll be lucky if I survive this pill." I usually quit reading the provided information, afraid to discover that continued use will make me disrupt meetings, disrespect my elders, and shoplift.

I also worry that the new pill I'm about to swallow will cause physical reactions that will require more pills, and then those pills will spur the need for more, on and on and on, until I need a wheeled suitcase to move my prescriptions from room to room.

Remembering when to take a pill, with what, and without what, is akin to memorizing *The Rhyme of the Ancient Mariner*—and as merry. How do you manage two pills you can't take together that need to be taken in the morning, on an empty stomach, one hour before eating, and four hours before consuming anything that contains calcium? I lie awake at night, puzzling the impossible.

I frequently forget to take pills at mealtime. I'm distracted by my cooking: dropping ingredients on the floor, burning holes in hot pads, and wondering if I can substitute mashed beets for tomato paste. I don't mind, though. Forgetting to swallow a pill with dinner means I can take it later with a snack—though doing so will interfere with the bedtime pill that should be taken on an empty stomach.

Which reminds me, when the directions say to "Take with food," how much food does that mean? A cherry tomato or a generous piece of cheesecake?

The cost of pills can be dismaying; so dropping one on the floor initiates a search requiring a flashlight, the hand-patting of carpet, and my behind in the air while I sight along the floor. When I find the elusive capsule under the couch, nestled with dust, a decaying grape, and a lost sock, I worry about taking something found in such unsanitary conditions. Then I remember its cost and swallow.

Despite my unease about pills, I admit my life is better because of them. I spent many years with an ulcer: chugging milk, avoiding spicy foods, and telling doctors, "I am NOT stressed." Then a specialist prescribed a daily pill that controlled my symptoms; and a few years later, a three-week course of antibiotics that rid me of my ulcer. Not a day goes by that I'm not grateful.

More recently, thyroid medication stabilized my life, though I had my usual stormy relationship with the new pill: resistance, denial, anger, frothing. At one point, forgetting my degree was in education, not medicine, I decided I didn't really need to take the thing. A few months of weight gain, heart palpitations, muscle aches, and edginess, convinced me I needed it. My doctor, being kind, didn't lecture me.

I have been blessed by modern medications. I just hate taking them.

Epilogue Moving Into Winter

All my life, I've lived with the rhythm of seasons: the challenges met, the losses suffered, and the satisfactions realized in the life-affirming newness of spring, the energetic fullness of summer, the gentle fading of fall, and the uncompromising realities of winter.

In 2011, a few months before my sixty-ninth birthday, Joel and I decided to climb Huron Peak near Buena Vista, a Class 2 summit in the heart of the Sawatch. I worried as we finalized our plans, fearing I'd wear out when the trail became strenuous, and Joel would have to roll me back to the truck.

In the preceding decade, I'd climbed other fourteeners with vigor and enjoyment, experiencing only brief moments of minor hysteria. Recently, however, during less challenging hikes, diminished energy and sore knees had reminded me of my dad's song about the old gray mare that "ain't what she used to be."

I managed to banish my concerns as Joel and I started our climb on a promising day in August. My spirits soared, buoyed by the beauty of daybreak in the mountains and the companionship of my husband: a bond unharmed by our drive through an obliterating darkness to the trailhead on a rugged donkey path during which I miss-navigated two turns, and Joel used profanity.

Gradually, our rhythmic walk, buffeted by cool morning air,

became a prolonged series of steep switchbacks, causing us to slow our pace and shed our jackets. Later, when the path leveled and led us through a high mountain meadow filled with flowers and bird song under a blue-bowl sky, I felt fully alive. Then the trail changed abruptly: we began the belabored breathing and cautious foot placement of the final ascent to Huron's narrow, wind-blown summit, where we rested and exclaimed at the top-of-the-world view before starting down. As always, the descent surprised me with its length, steepness, and lack of charity toward my vulnerable knees.

A year later in 2012, as I turned seventy, the tics and twinges of my aging body had become outright complaints, and my optimistic outlook had altered as well: I found myself re-evaluating both my physical capabilities and my unthinking optimism about the future.

I've always enjoyed my birthdays, reflecting on the mostly good life I've lived and the relationships I've enjoyed, looking forward to many years ahead. But this birthday was different. For the first time I saw my life as limited. I understood that it must end on a future date within my imagining. It is no longer so far in the future that it seems forever.

When young, I yearned to be older, took risks, and denied my mortality. During my middle years, I became more realistic about my age, but played a comforting game. As November 9th neared, I'd think: "So, I'll be turning fifty; if I make it to ninety, I'll live forty more years. That's forever."

Then at sixty, I thought, "Hmm. If I make it to ninety, I still have thirty years ahead of me. I've a lot of living left to do."

But as I turned seventy, I realized that ninety was twenty years away, and the last twenty have passed in a flash, seeming to take no time at all. So I wrestled with my new, fully realized understanding: life is finite; I can no longer rely on endless tomorrows.

Some readers may wonder why it took me so long to grasp this basic concept; others may shake their heads at my foolishness for wasting time thinking about it. I suppose the recognition of our mortality arrives for each of us at its own pace. It turned up on my doorstep on a fall-turning-to-winter day as leaves blossomed to a vivid yellow; the Yampa River dwindled to a lazy stream; and I contemplated my seventieth birthday.

CPSIA information can be obtained at www.ICGtesting.com
Printed in the USA
LVOW11s0707140214

373459LV00002BA/144/P